Ponderings and Pictures

Vol. 6

Dallas Dixon

ISBN: 979-8-3483-4802-1

Interior design and cover design:
Deborah Perdue: www.illuminationgraphics.com

2024 Linked In postings by Dallas Dixon,
Dementia Dude

Dedication

To my wife, daughters and daughter in law
and to Nate, Adelaide and family.

And may your spirits know the fullness of joy.

The Dementia Declaration of Independence

1. We, the people living with dementia, our friends, family, caregivers and supporters, no longer accept the dying vegetable label. Nor do we condone the use of this and other false narratives by organizations for their purposes.

2. We declare that folks with dementia have a super power that protects certain joys from cognitive decline: music appreciation, the delight of play, deep love, spiritual memory, a sense of humor, the ability to read tones of voice and numerous and various artistic expressions which include painting, poetry, woodworking, gardening, dance, bird watching and many others.

3. We declare these joys to be self-evident. They are our right in our pursuit of happiness, joy and safety. It is our personal and corporate expectation whatever setting we are in.

From the dementia dudes and dudettes around the world

Late picking you up from school.
As you struggle to download
an overflowing bookbag over
the twiggy shoulders, you perk
up for assurances unspoken.

My smile uploads across

time to land softly in my spirit
tonight and again tomorrow.
4/27/24

If you have dementia and are bored
something or someone is getting in the way of real joy.

Who says we dementia people can't bear regular people
with gentleness,
long suffering and in love?

One of the coolest things about dementia is when you
order online you get two of what you order.

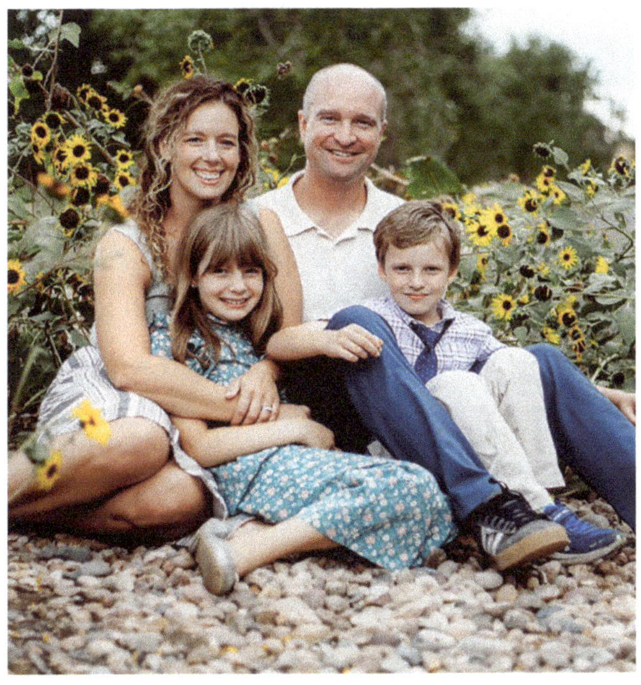

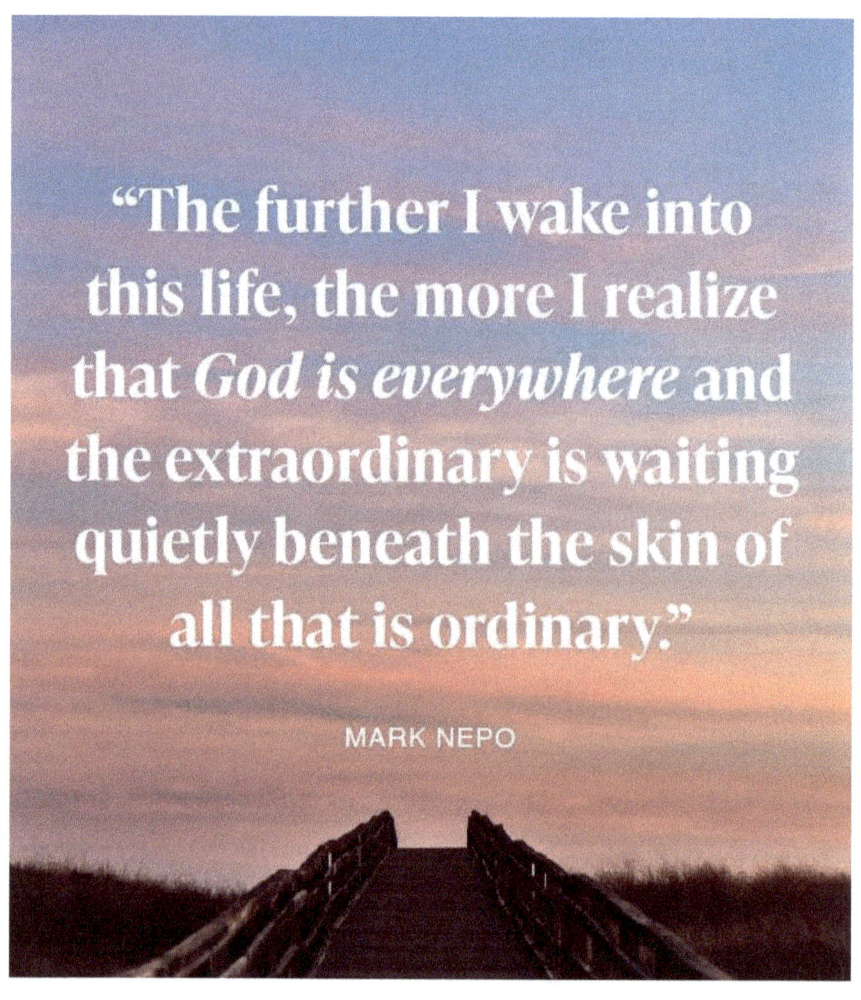

From a bunch of stuff (dementia, obesity, pacemaker) my body is a mess. But my soul is renovated and my spirit is supplemented.

Joy vs. happiness? Joy for me has been elusive until I knew the spirit of being forgiven for following my own path.

LinkedIn has gotten too hard, too fast.
So I'm going to working with poetry
because it lets me be comfortable.

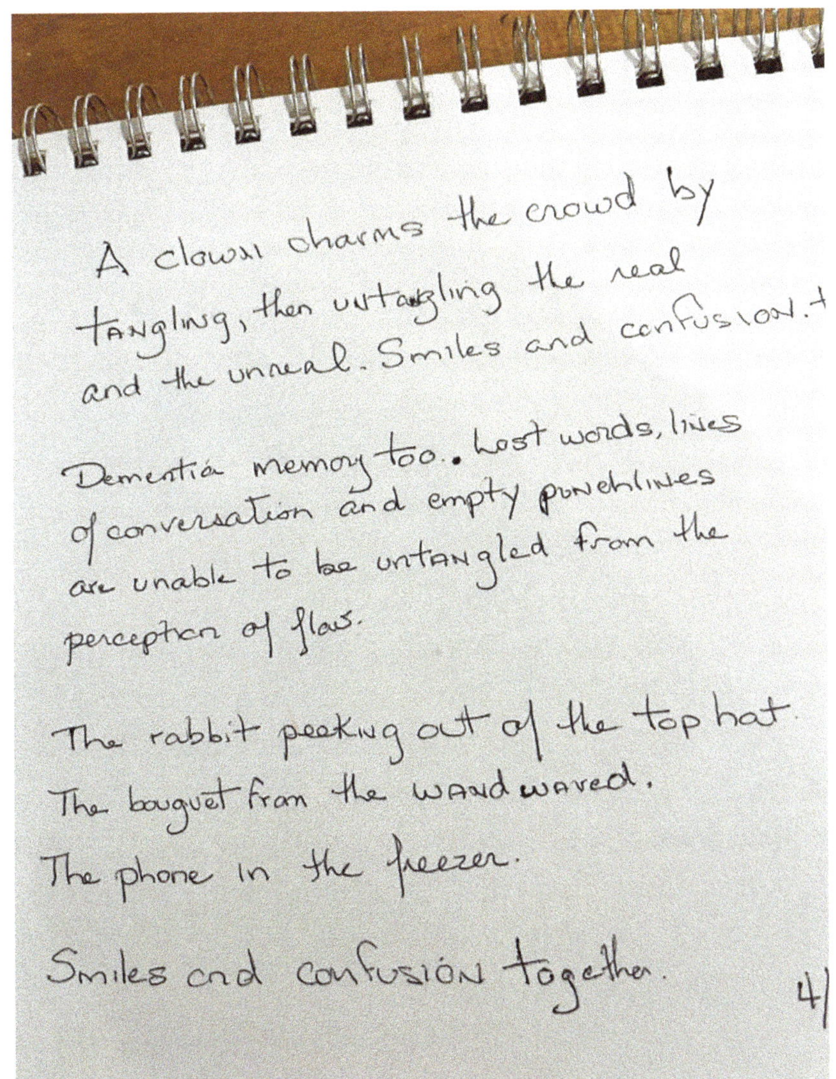

Michelle Olson…Oliver James…Alma Valencia…Macie P. Smith…James Vickers…Bii Yates…Norman Rockwell…Graeme Atkins…Jacqui Bingham…Charles Bronson…Sean Connery…Peter Bery…Nina Balackova…Veda Meneghetti…David Cassidy…Trach Shorthouse…Myrna Norman…Minna…Charlton Heston…Jeff Borghoff…Marianne Benz…Arlene Francis…Eddie Albert…Maria Turner…Arlene Francis…Gwendolyn de Geest…John McErlane…Nigel Hula…Bill Quackenbush…Russel Forster…Judy Cornish…Otto Preminger…Margaret Thatcher…Gordie Howe…Burgess Meredith…Wendy Mitchell…Paula Wolford…Amy Spring…Jay Reinstein. "bank manager" Norman McNamara…Cheryl Harding…Sonya Barsness...@Dementia folks in jail…Christine Thelker…Eileen Taylor…Chris Roberts…Helga Rohra…John Quinn…Brian Van Buren…Jacqueline Wong…Peter Mittler…Angie Li…Terri Montgomery…John Sandblom…Mike Belleville…Mark Roberts…Nancy McArden…Barney Nelson…Jim Mann…Joanna Fix…Brenda Roberts…Cameron Camp…Dr. Eva van der Ploeg…Katie Norris…Jaqueline Revere…Gertrude Jordan…Patrick Ettenes…Brenda Wilson…Oliver James…Jessica Cannon…Erinne Stewart…Bill Yates…Linda Brewster…Janine Whited…Jaqueline Wong…Sally Faith…God. This is the 2nd of two lists of dementia heroes for 2024. Deadline Dec. 31, 2023. Additions or edits can be made here. Questions here too.

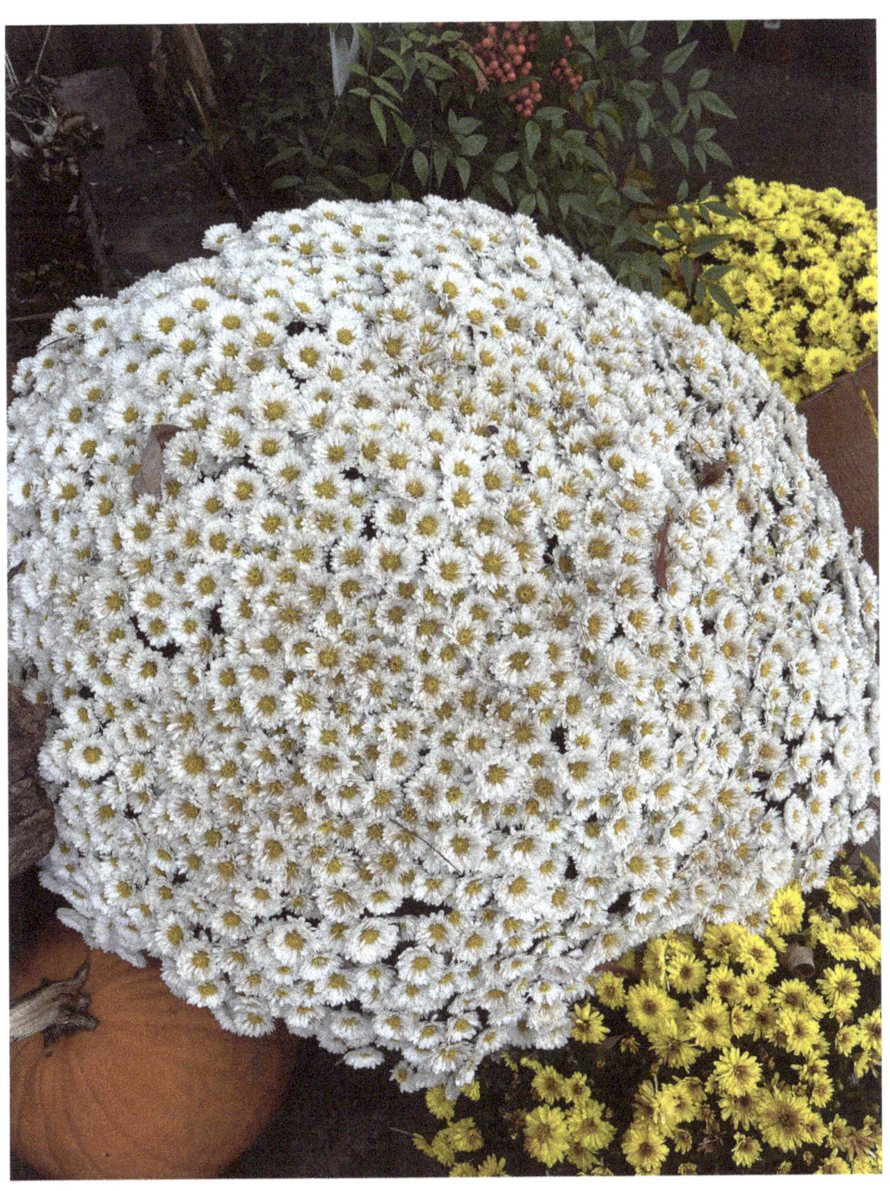

The intuitive world feels like a pillow for my head. Cognition is overrated.

To Regulars.

Please:

1. Don't ask how we are doing.

2. Don't ask what we did today.

3. Don't interrupt.

4. No long stories.

5. No quick changes in subjects.

6. No background noise competition.

7. No baby.

8. Don't say just write it down.

9. No arguing.

10. No "don't you remember…"

PS. I was a caregiver for 10 years before dementia so I messed up regularly too.

Keep trying.

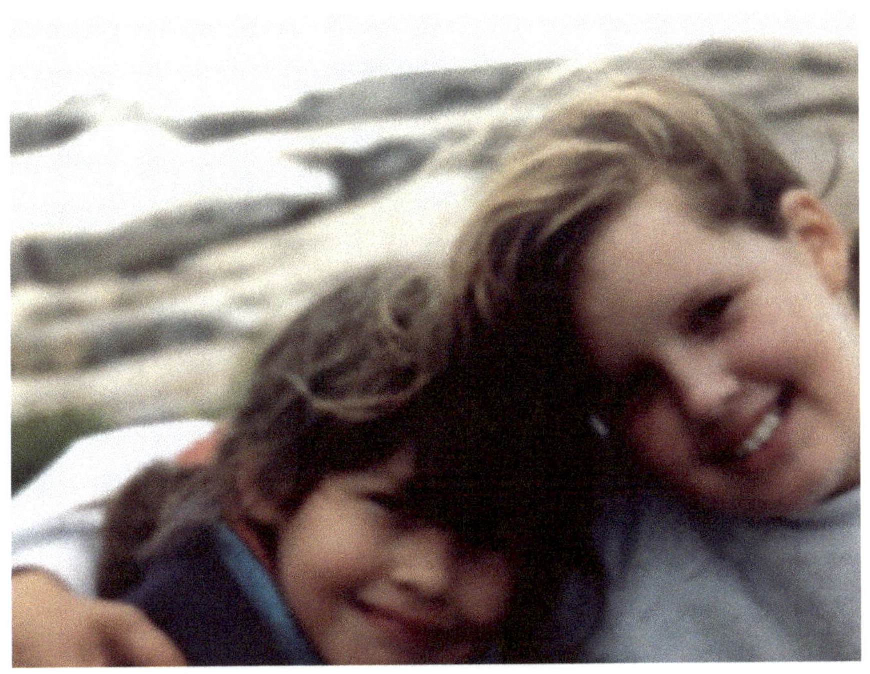

Picking up your young kids from school,
struggling with their backpacks, peeking up to grab
assurances unspoken, can bring a warm smile
50 years later.

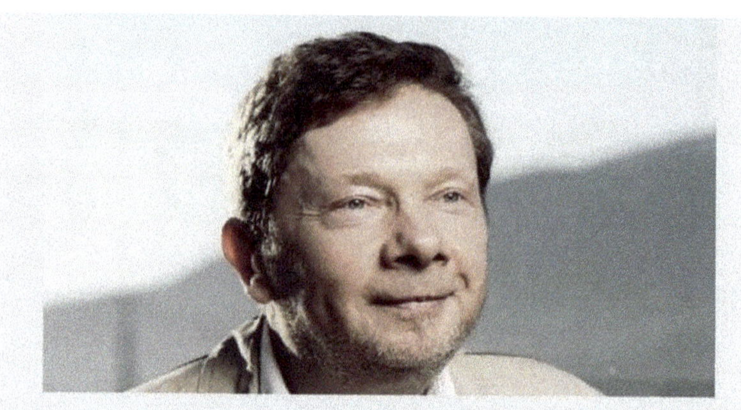

You know what surprises me about having

dementia? Regulars are angry that we have

dementia. They pretend to get it,

but they really don't.

The buttons are coming undone.

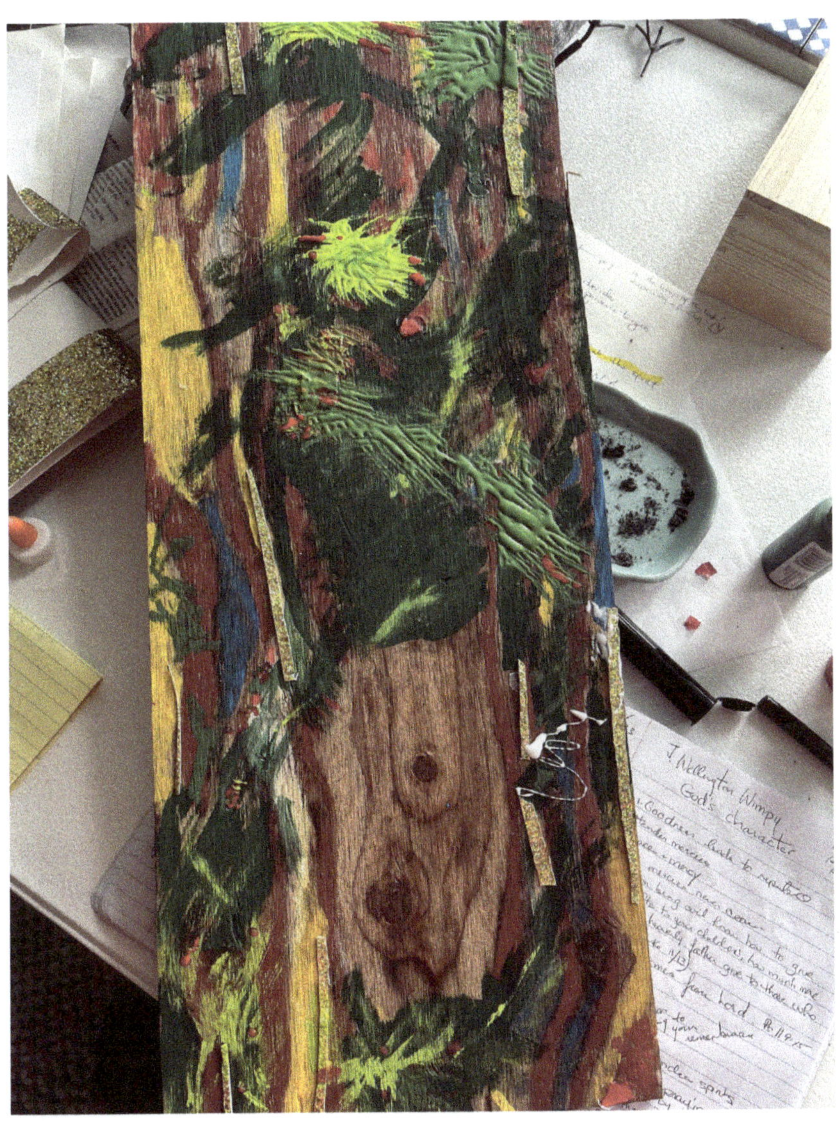

11

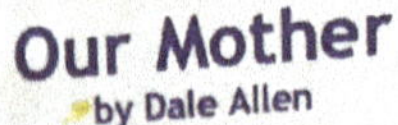

Our Mother
by Dale Allen

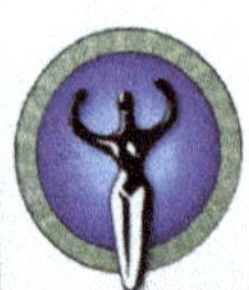

Our Mother who art within us
Each breath brings us to you.
Thy wisdom come,
Thy will be done
as we honor your presence within us.
You give us this day all that we need.
Your bounty calls us to give and receive
all that is loving and pleasurable.
You are the courage that moves us
to be true to ourselves
and we act with grace and power.
We relax into your cycles of
birth, growth, death, and renewal.
Out of the womb, the darkness, the void,
comes new life.
For you are the Mother of All Things.
Your body is the Sacred Earth
and our bodies.
Your love nurtures us and unites us all.
Now and forever more.

www.inourrightminds.net

Thy wisdom come,

Thy will be done.

I mean it's one thing not liking us dementia folk because you are afraid of dementia. It's another thing to purposely try to get over on us to exploit us financially (aka steal from us or worse).

DEMENTIA. Tidbit. Most of the time I want to do the right thing. It is worth 0, because it was all for me to show off outside and inside. I say this to prove you wrong about dementia Get over it. Dementia is more…like a new language. Learn it and it will be fun.

Don't you think it's funny that I feel a need to explain to regulars that I have dementia? Cancer not so much and a scar or tattoo not at all.

Ah. It's my turn for the dementia real dreams (aka terror dreams). They are quite the experience. Mine are in the courtroom or in the street. Maybe God's way of getting rid of the sludge (aka the sh- -). Share them to assure complete ejection.

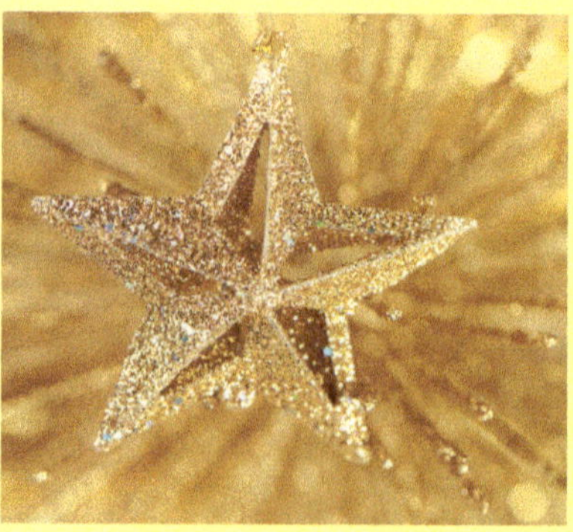

I'm not saying that dementia creates a new spirituality.

I'm saying it doesn't get in the way, maybe it's good soil.

God speaks to me and I take no credit, only joy.

God knows my name and I take no credit, only joy.

And dementia plays no part, God's grace and mercy is
the only star.

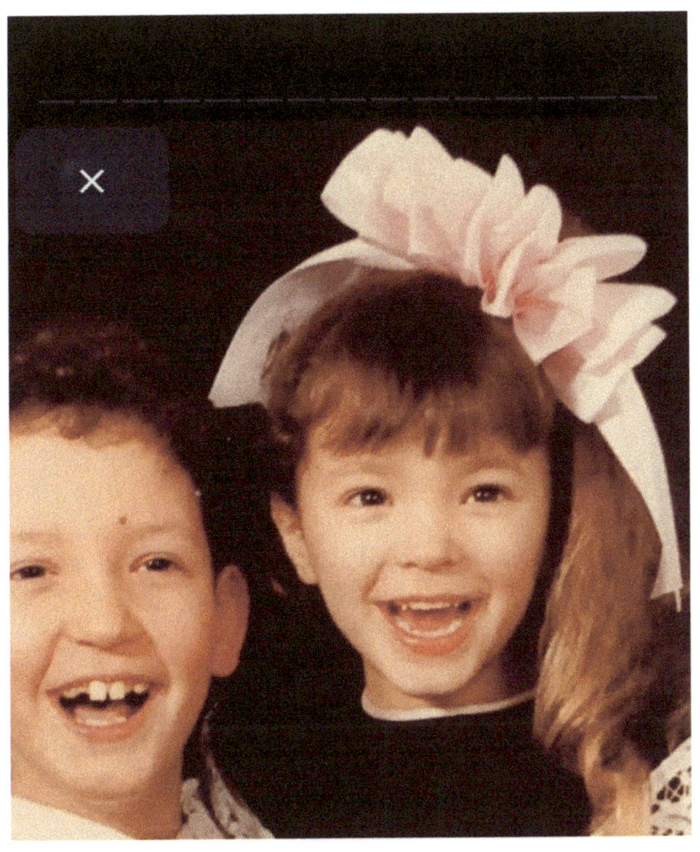

Dementia is for the birds. Ain't it grand?

Just sayin'. I think grace and mercy is God's go-to bread and butter; it has purpose in our dementia world. Let me think on it.

Guard your heart above all else, for it determines the course of your life.

Proverbs 4:23 (NLT)

So if I remember much of my kindergarten class and I forget about what day it is, doesn't it mean my memories are here, but the recovery of them is not so much?

This dementia dude remembers two names but I remember what I felt toward each individual and teacher. I got the better in the trade.

EVERYONE with dementia should have a job they like.

Raising awareness of dementia serves no purpose if raising awareness doesn't include the truth about us instead of about misinformation for all of us. Boycott all Alz groups without a dementia person or two on their boards.

Raising awareness of dementia serves no purpose if raising awareness doesn't include the truth about us instead of about misinformation for all of us. Boycott all Alz groups without a dementia person or two on their boards.

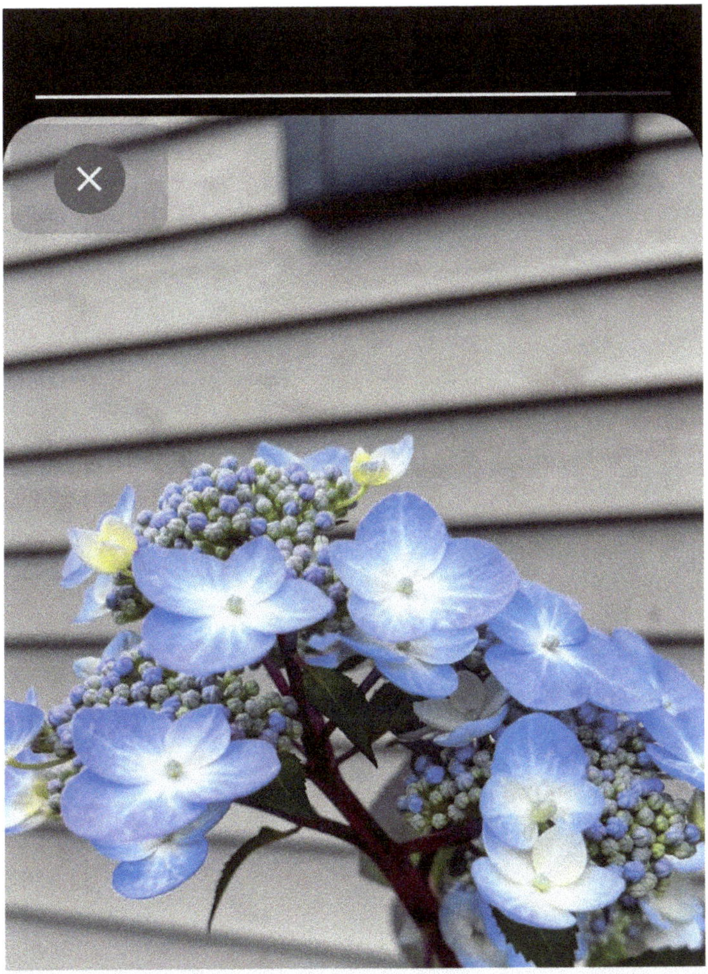

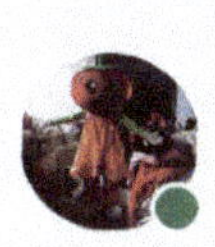

Dallas Dixon · You
Dementia author and wanna be dementia advocate and activist.
2d · 🌐

We must as dementia people surrender our cognitive side but must defend any trespass of our intuitive and spirit sides and just as importantly, 🙏 ❤️ our hearts.

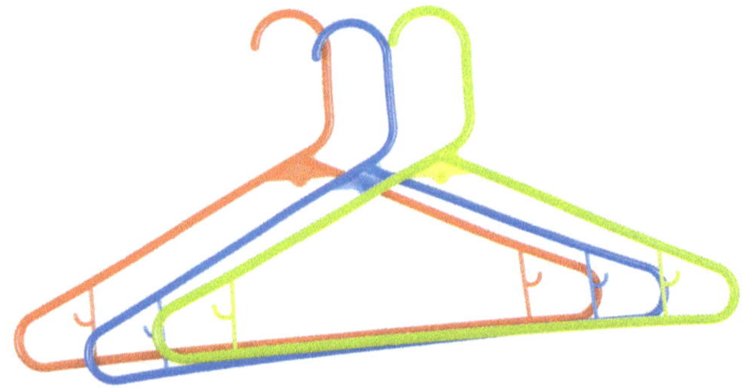

Dementia tidbit.

Hangers are way better than drawers.

Here is to a new week!

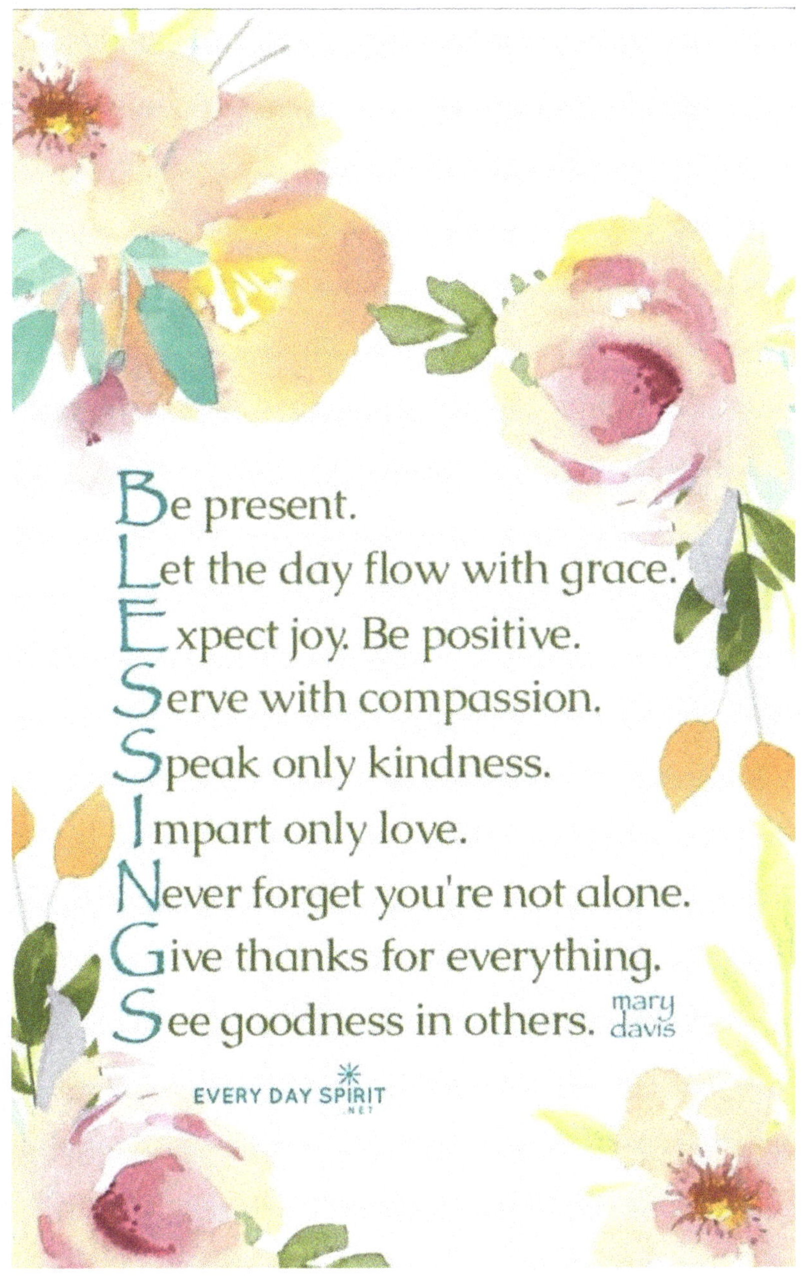

I've been very curious about why some regular people are very cold and angry at a dementia person…for no apparent reason. the three people in my life, I believe are afraid of dementia in a deeply personal way. They can be ruthlessly hypercritical. It must be hard.

No longer is the dilemma between caregivers and care partners. It is are you a joy maker? It's harder but way better than person centered, etc. Blech. Get out of our heads. Quit being a cognitive bully.
Let's giggle and hee haw.

The difference is that play takes up time, joy creates relationship, trust life.

Caregivers or care partners or activity directors can play but are they creating joy?

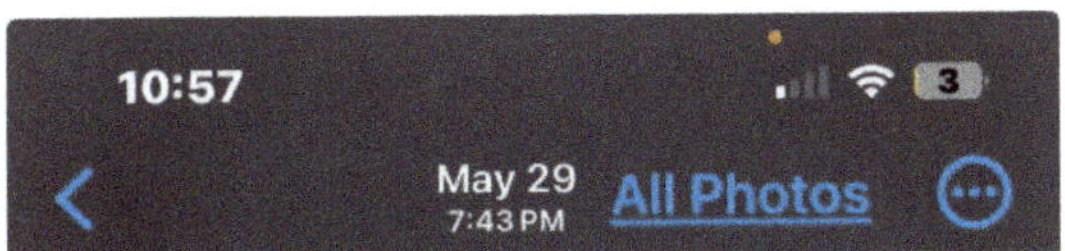

moment-by-moment thoughts and cognitive ponderings turn in undivided love to Him. It also brings us to an understanding that without Yeshua we can do nothing, but in Him we can do all things, including to love as He loved us thus allowing Him to live and work through us so that as His love shines through our life, and He be glorified through it. It is out of His deep and everlasting love for us that He commands this level of affection from His children, for it is only as our love is centered upon Him, that our lives will be transformed into His image and likeness. Only then will His perfect love flow through us to others. Loving the Lord with all our heart, and soul, and mind, and strength, is a progressive love that builds and develops in our Christian walk, for as we grow in grace and in a knowledge of our Lord and Savior, we are enabled to have that love translated into the good works that

If you never had the opportunity to learn to play,

get someone to teach you, without saying they need

to know.

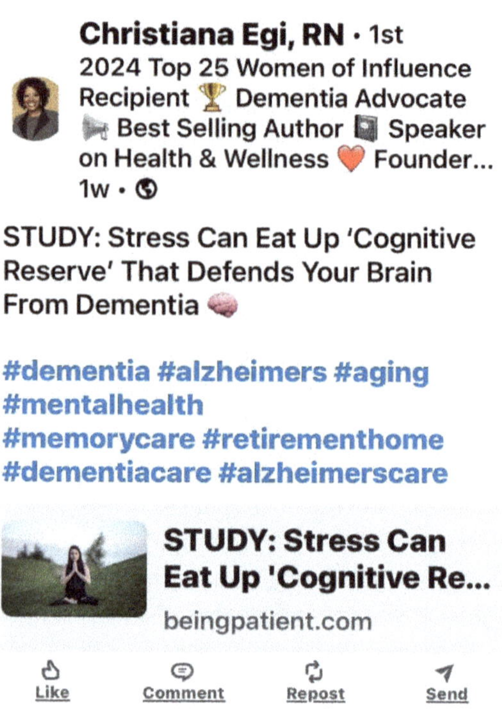

I was truly a basketball nut. Played 3–4 times a week with my boys. They called me Double D. I couldn't remember who was on my team. Sh…a problem. But when I cross paths with the asphalt, the heat that you can see…intoxicating…playing pickup for 10 minutes among the eventual NCAA champs. Thanks Johnnie Jones, Howard Porter, Sammy Sims, and that left-handed 3 when my right shoulder was on the mend. Oh yea. There was that time at 6 A.M. at the JCC where I couldn't miss. Really couldn't miss. For KB.

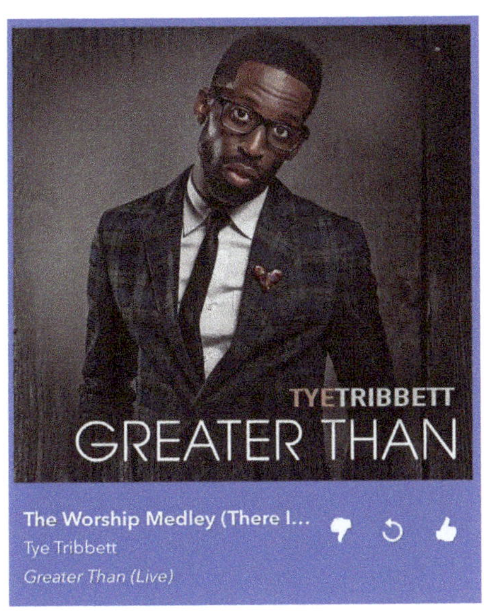

Doreen Lovell · 1st   ···   ✕
Author, Prayer intercessor
3h · 🌐

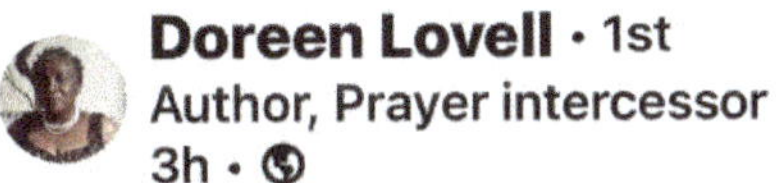

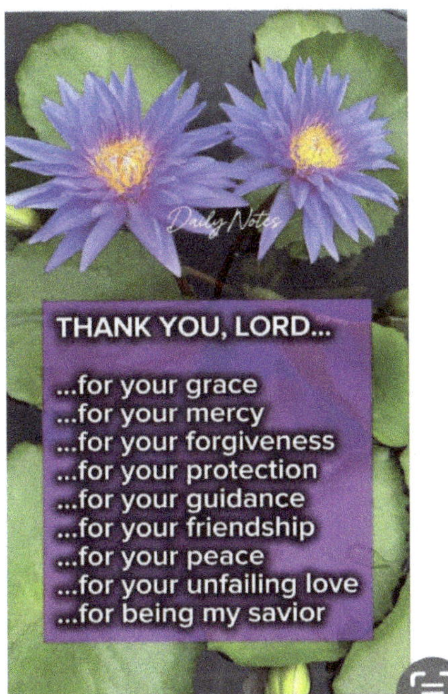

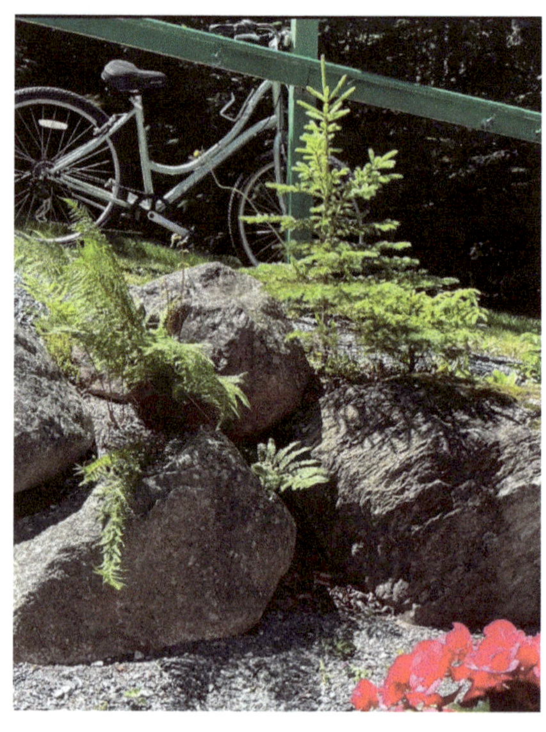

Before I forget, playing cards in bad lighting is rough but music is not, painting is not. Tv sucks, especially with the sound, telling stories or jokes is not. Family gatherings are awful. Chilling with my friends, smoking marijuana works.

A caregiver motivated primarily by obligation will be an unhappy camper. Motivated by love will have more moments of joy than we thought possible. Ah. But what is each of our definition of love? Not easily angered, patient, kind, doesn't insist on his own way…

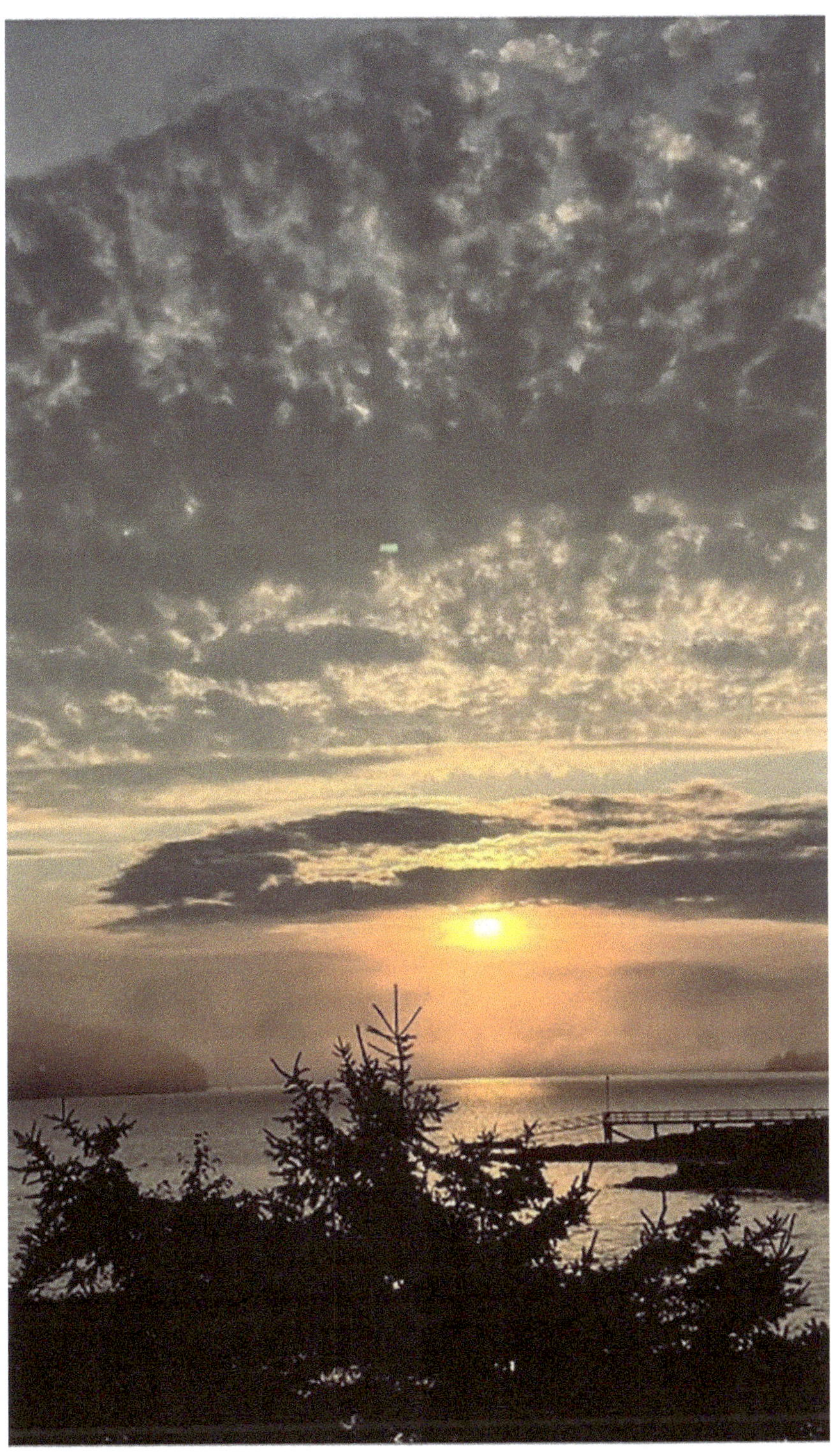

Dallas Dixon • You

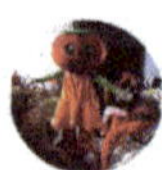

Dementia author and wanna be dementia advocate and activist.
now •

Mark5:36. Do not be afraid , only believe.Dementia translation:Do not be afraid of dementia.Only believe it carries no pain.Only believe that dementia can be your friend.

👍 **Like**   💬 **Comment**

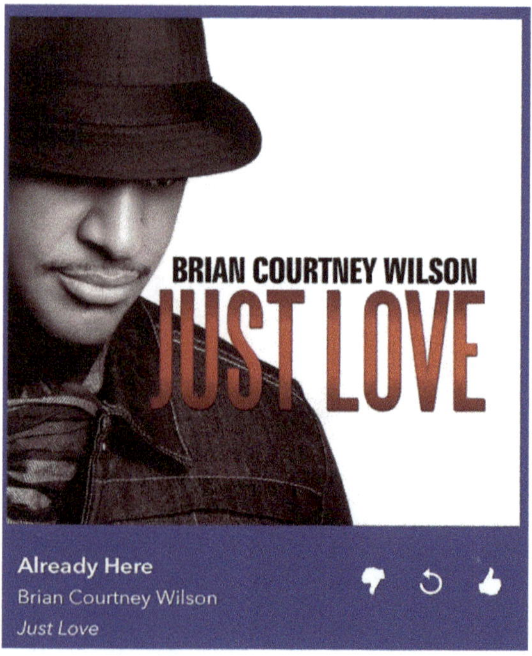

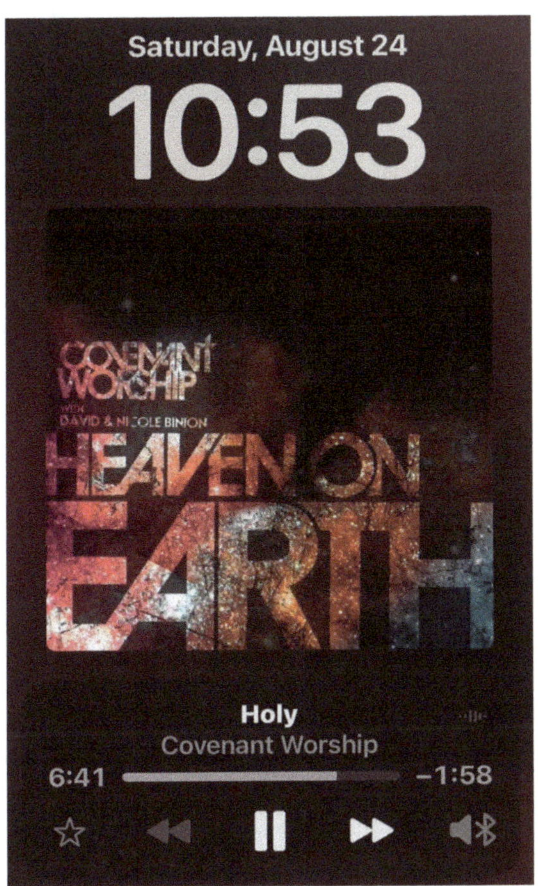

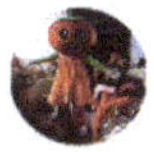 **Dallas Dixon** · You
Dementia author and wanna be dementia advocate and activist.
3w ·

There is a d groove where the world is in balance with a shrinking brain.Nice moments.Caregivers not allowed probably.

 2

For years I thought it was mostly, if not all, me and my dementia causing chaos. But there are a lot of dementia people haters who reflect this same narrative…shaming…rolling eyes…nasty tones about how many times we asked the same question…It's all about the haters being afraid of dementia for themselves.

Bravo x 10.

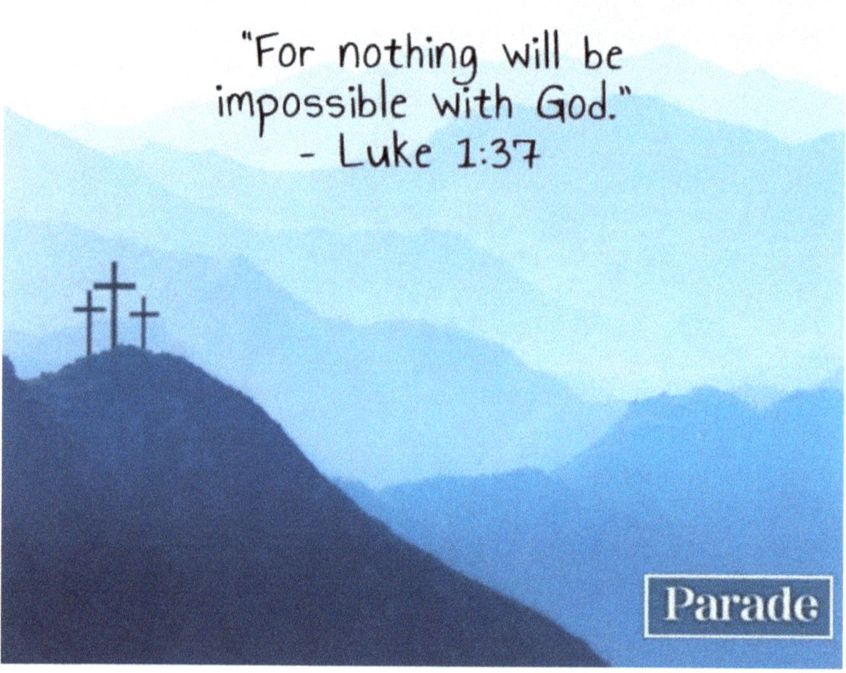

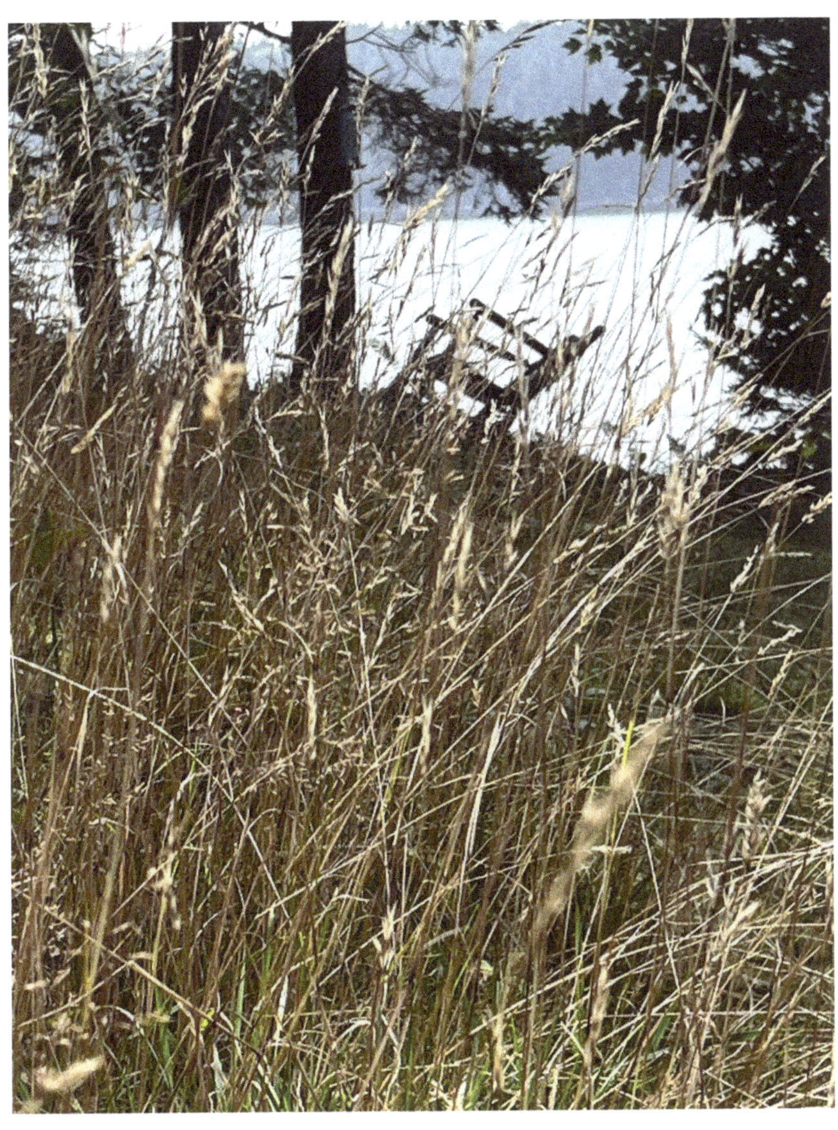

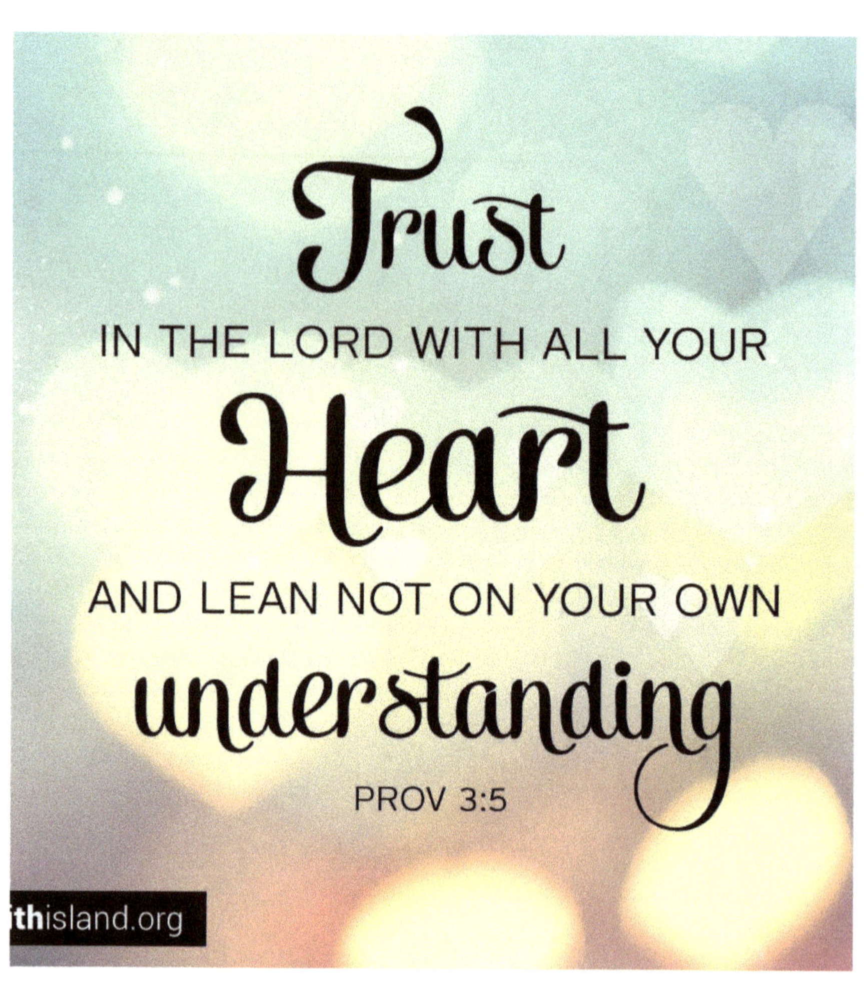

FAITH AND TRUST

IN THE LORD ALWAYS

Dementia trainers need to check out you—
our dementia and old people prejudice…
ingrained deeply. Often dealing with our own
experiences with our old people and family.
My first was doc. A science buff he drank milk
and sugar every meal due to being gassed in
WW1. A mixture of feelings. Most prominent
was wanting to defend him when he was being
dogged. He knew it was a small thing, it was no
bother.

Watching tv all day is negligent care.
Overtime…abusive. We don't know what we
are watching. Don't tell staff. We are hiding
from the guards. Wish I was all the way deaf.
Better leverage.

If you make fun of a regular, and they know u
have dementia, check for any visible p e d.

I was hitchhiking last summer, and a colleague
stopped, concerned I was "wandering in the
dementia sense."

I'm pretty sure that dealing with
dementia is different than dealing with
death. But do death and dementia
interact?

They have all these weird descriptions of
our dementia stages. Simplify, simplify.
Try the major stages: death and not
death. Or better yet…the amount of
times I've left the refrigerator door open
for 30 minutes or more (5 or 6).

I root for Bonnie and Clyde. If they catch
them, lights out. If they find out about
my incontinence, off to the memory unit.
Favorite movie: The Great Escape.

Kate.

Boycott Alzheimer's groups. Mostly no
dementia people on their boards and
they don't even know how
to talk dementia.

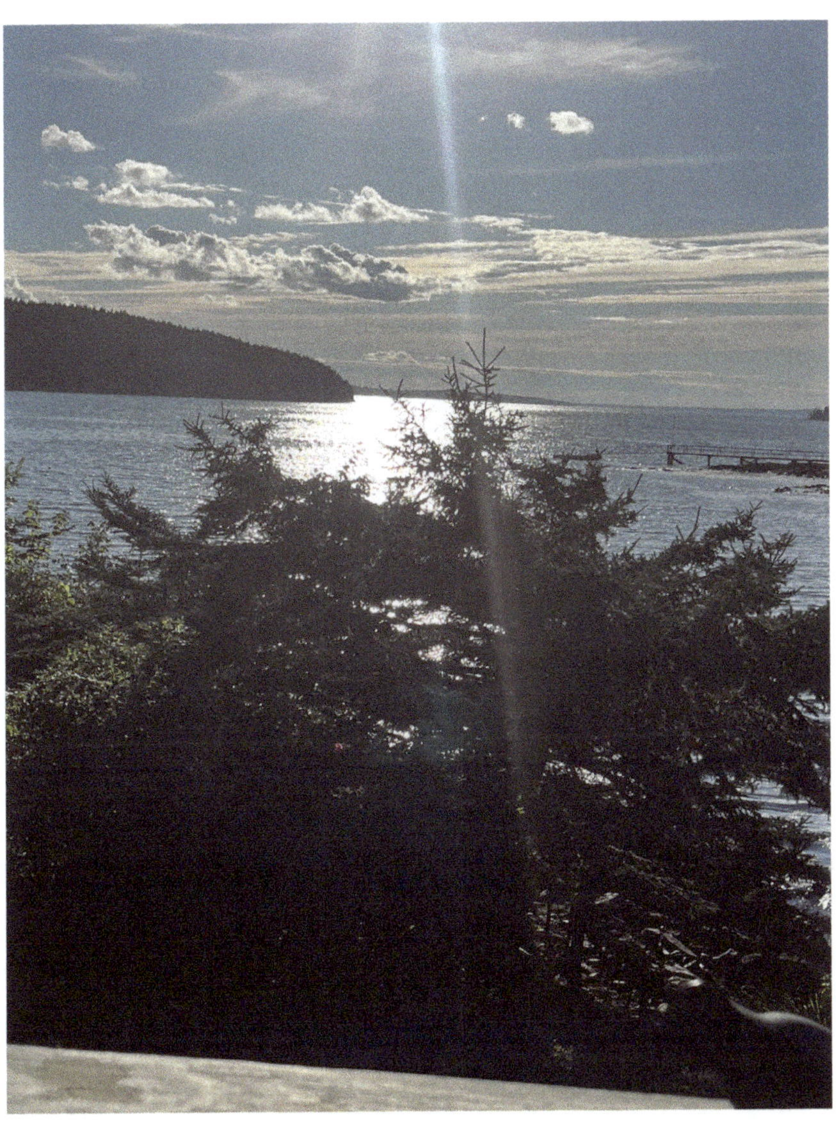

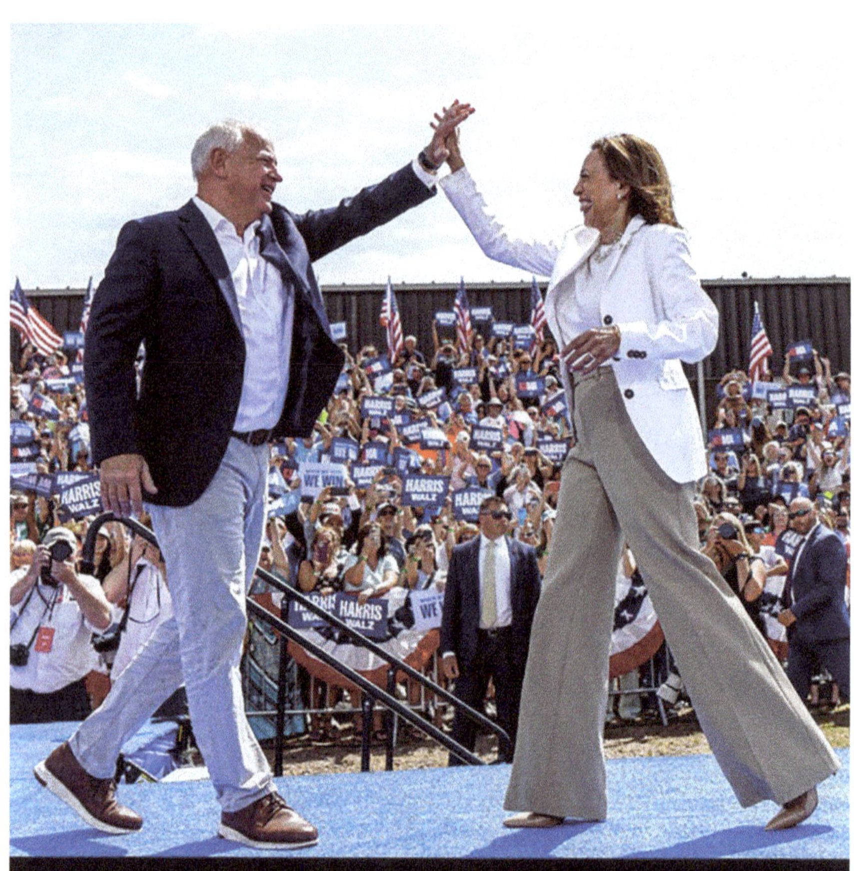

Kerem Yücel/Minnesota Public Radio, via Associated Press

All caregivers should be paid even with a hand rub.
No rub, no care, lol.

I have never met (including me) anyone in my neighborhood who wasn't a tad racist. But Trump is like the guy who eats 50 plus hotdogs at one sitting.

Don't worry. Nicki and Nancy…sound sorta alike. Like New Hampshire and New York.

Two dementia worries. 1. If Trump can mimic physical disability in front of millions, what is he going to do to demean us? 2. Who is preparing for this now?

Kamala Harris and Tim Walz.

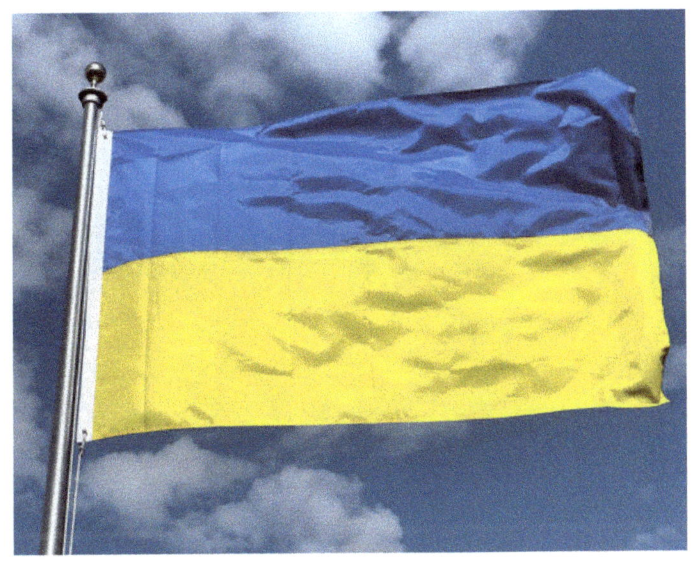

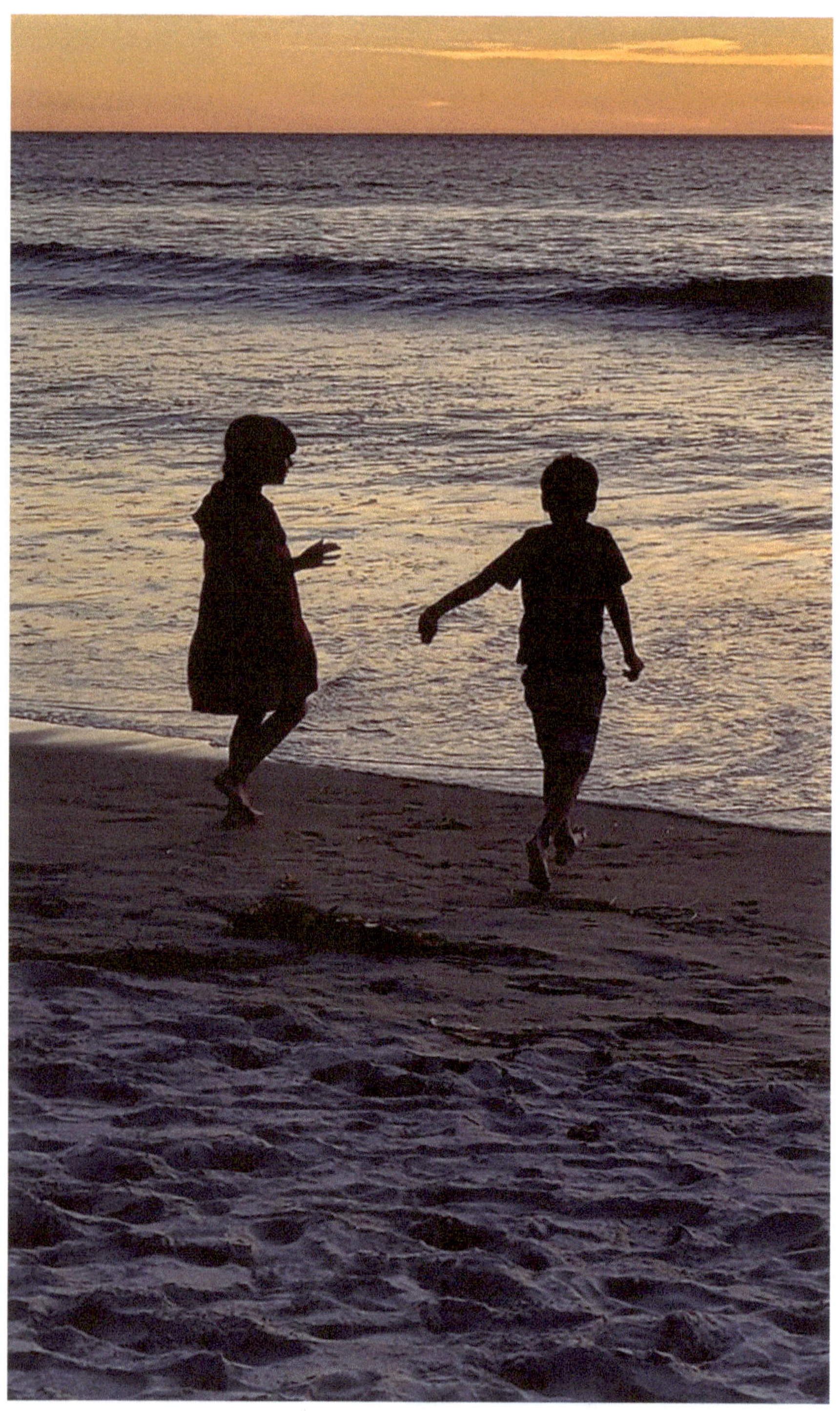

1% milk. But brain and soul. Sucking still.
Like binge watching.

The tv sedative would not cause too much harm except when it starts to suck out your soul. Carers see it as re-spite. We can all do better…including us d's.

Had a dementia altercation. I was explaining my need to go a little slower, which created nose up. So I asked the security officer to join me in a little talk with the manager. If not the security guy, the blame is going to slide downhill. I said that this is the second time at your marijuana store where I was ghosted. I need your card because if this happens again, never coming back and will letter to editor. Lambertville, NJ.

The only way our dementia system, which
is built on 1900s lies of regular people, gets
better is through us.

Our God doesn't stop running after us just
because we have dementia. (chuckle)

It's trouble in d3land. I say goodbye to too
complicated tv. It's sorta like the stove fire.
No mas.
Gotta draw a line.

On the basketball courts my name was
Double D.
I really hate the word dementia.
Way wrong vibe.
So I suggest we call ourselves d. for
dementiafried.
Now I'm triple d. Yeah, man.

We both needed therapy.

Where have ye gone, Harry?

Processing.

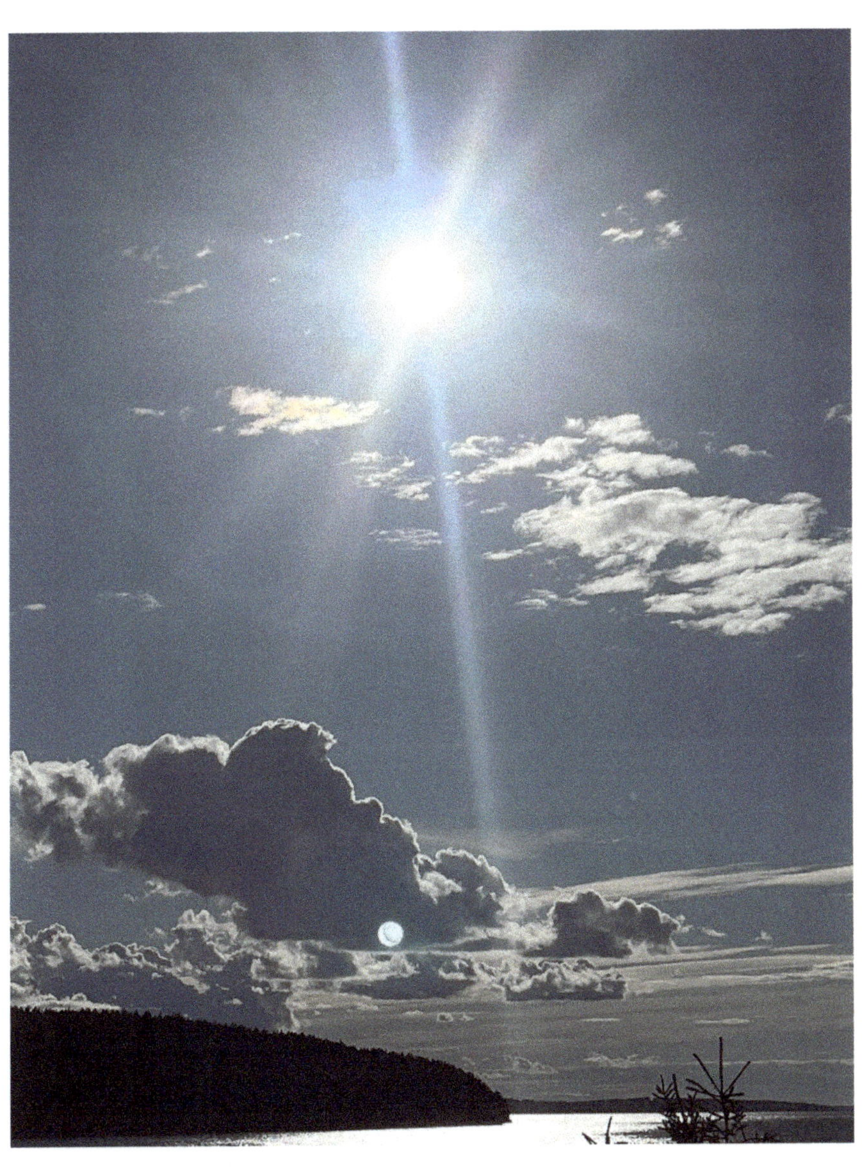

Our God doesn't stop running after us
just because we have dementia.
(chuckle)

> But from there you
> will search again
> for the LORD your
> God. And if you
> search for Him
> with all your heart
> and soul, you will
> find Him.
>
> Deuteronomy 4:29 (NLT) Read Full
> Chapter

Regulars and light impact d people try to bullshit us because they think they are quicker. Maybe yes maybe no. But they think with a twist of the tongue or facial deception, they can fool us for their benefit.

That's nasty…shit.

So we need to train us in how to handle fdp regulars. I've been thrown out of 2 1/2 doctors' offices and today essentially out of marijuana. SEE. Always ask an independent sort or a security guard to witness your complaint of their rudeness of us. They won't believe us.

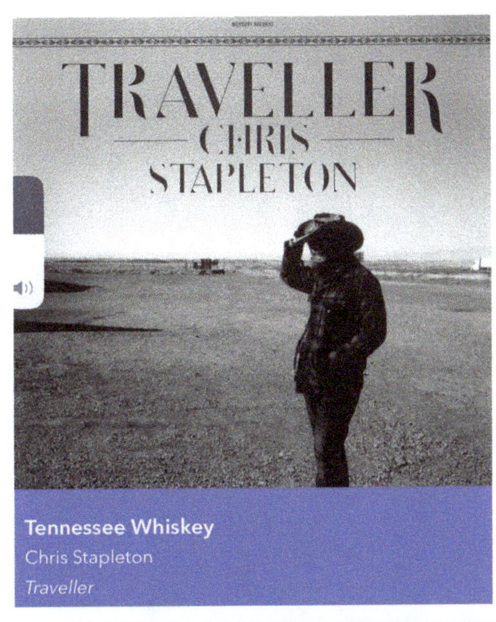

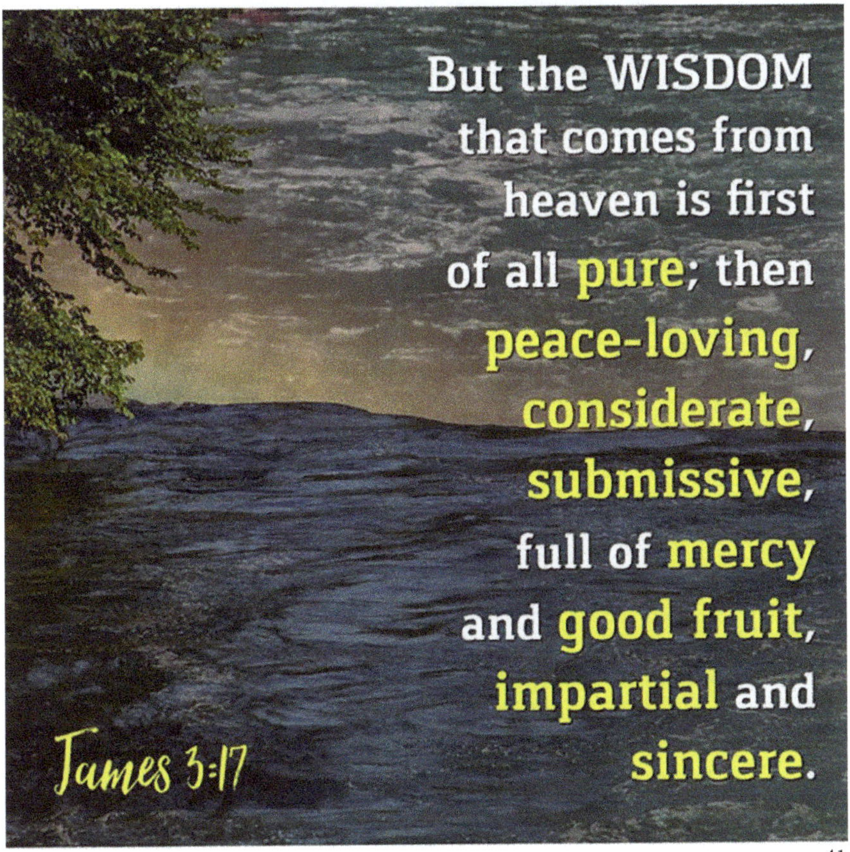

But the WISDOM that comes from heaven is first of all pure; then peace-loving, considerate, submissive, full of mercy and good fruit, impartial and sincere.

James 3:17

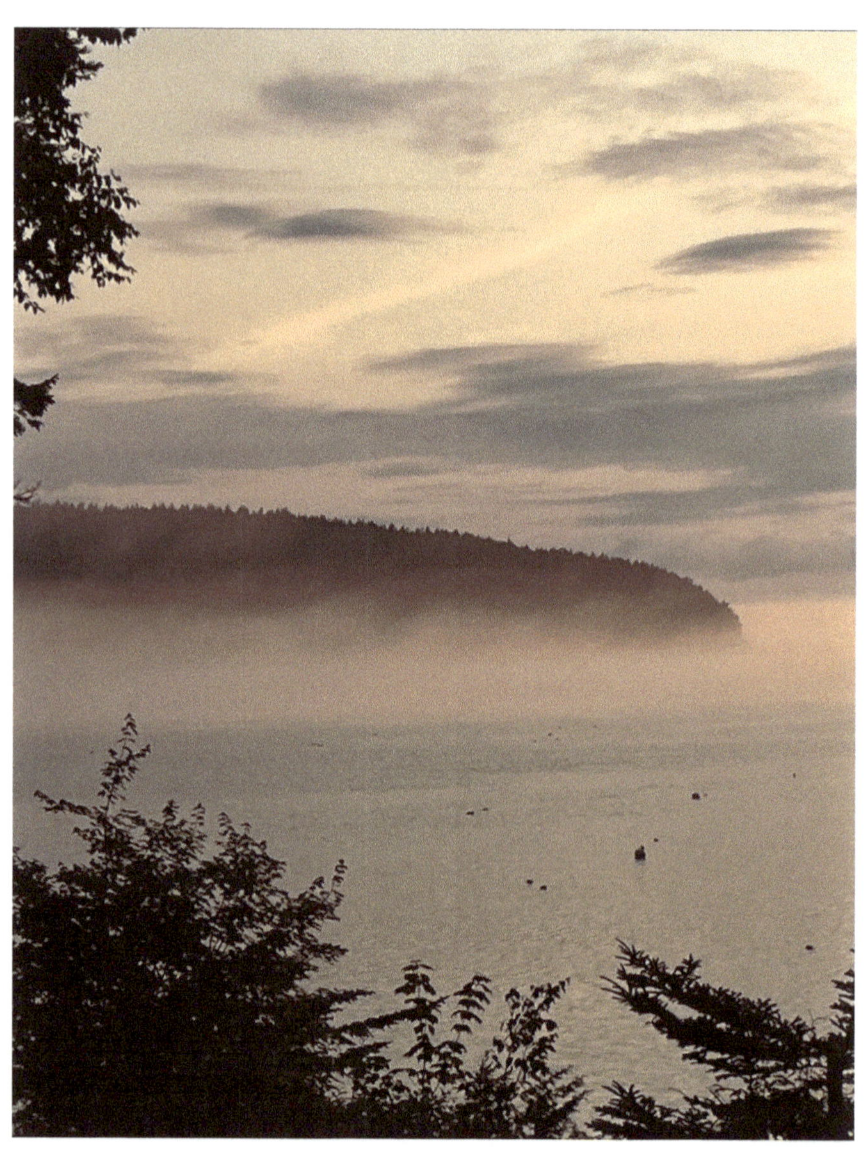

So, please tell me in simple terms the relationship
between Alexa and Dementia, especially in
dementiafried times? Need help here.
Drip some sympathy over here.

Who is the best teacher of dementia?

Me plus 100 other dementia dudes and dudettes.

Emily Ong is a leader in this dementia world. Brilliant.

Top 10 Dementia Hits

#10   God restores what has been lost and broken.

#9   Eat half, walk double, laugh triple, and give and accept love without measure.

#8   Dementia creates a door to the intuitive world.

#7   God wil bring to your remembrance all the things he has said to you.

#6   Dementia protects joys from cognitive decline.

#5   God renews our strength.

#4   Dementia is being and experiencing, not knowing and doing.

#3   Wisdom can be found by asking God without doubting.

#2   Sense of humor, music, the arts and more are gifts of dementia.

#1   All of us dementia folks are entitled to know each of these Top 10 and others no matter the setting, the brand of dementia or the cognitive progression.

Always be joyful. Never stop praying.

1 Thessalonians 5:16-17 NLT

L o v e.

Forgetting is underrated.

Fun.

Having fun.

*"He who kisses the joy as it flies lives
in Eternity's sunrise."*
Steven Mitchell

I savor joy, I rejoice in joy, I find joy
in the simplest things.

And when I'm not feeling it, I go to what I can rely
on to lift my mood, and that is to recount what I am
grateful for.

Joy is always within me, even when I have to coax it out.

And how grand to know that when I kiss it, I am
dwelling in the beauty of eternity.

Deborah Perdue, Gratitude Gal

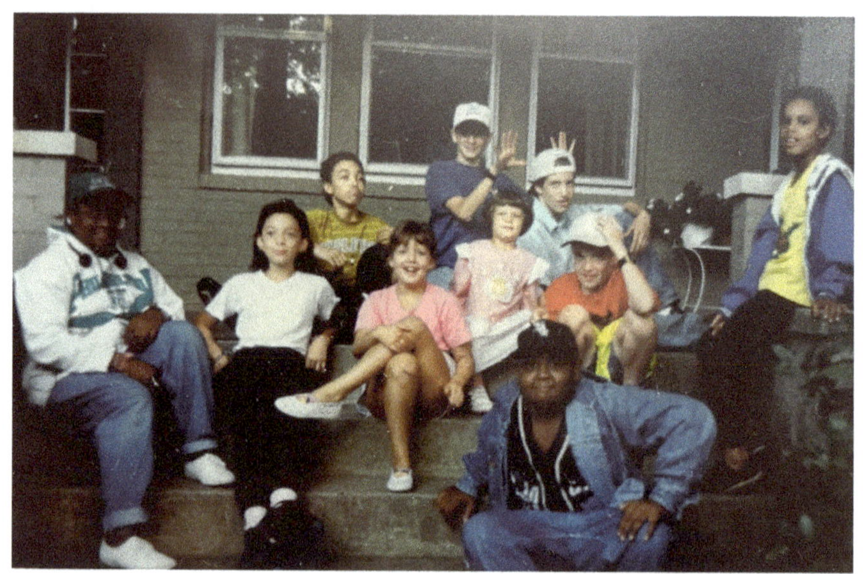

Dancing dementia dude was meant to honor Christine Bryden, the dementia avatar. Her book Dancing with Dementia was my first hope book. Ddd. Today, tho, was the first day I felt like I was.

My advice is please don't demonize dementia. From prez down to me.

Joy

Heals and Uplifts!

The genesis of regular people bullying is selfishness, of course. But it is manifested often around you defining time for yourself, not us. Talk too slowly…think too slowly…eat too slowly. Use the bathroom too slowly. Get in the car too slowly. Be affectionate too slowly. Understand too slowly. If you can't slow down with us, get another job…never too quickly.

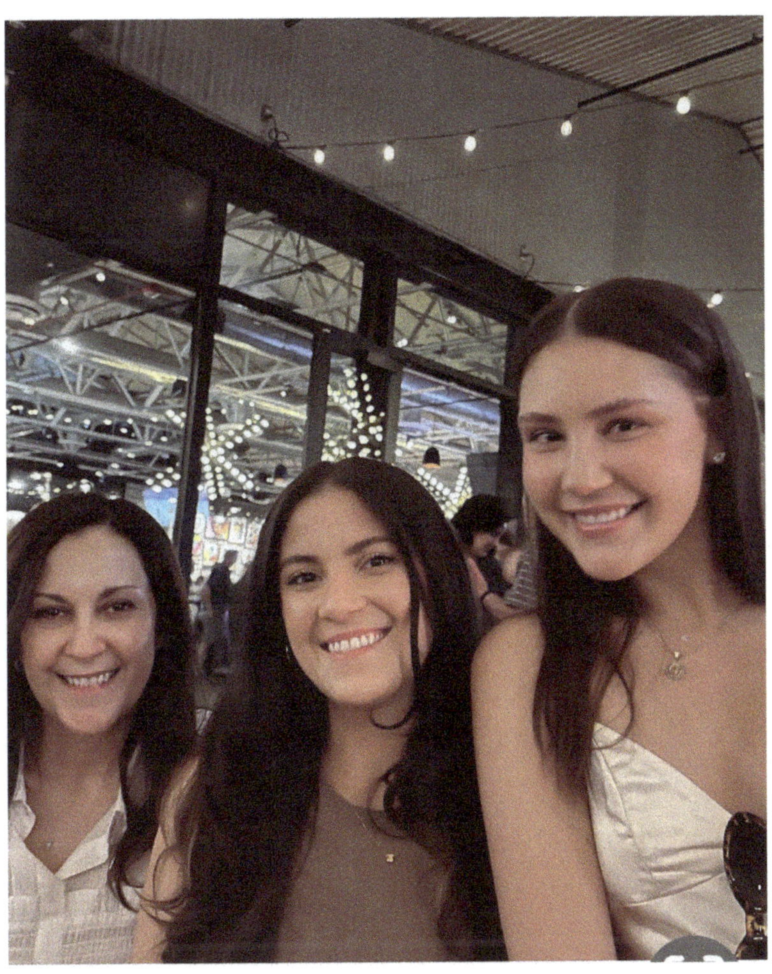

Can't fight the forget. Enjoy fun.

One second faster than myself.
We take a while to process. Be patient or go home.

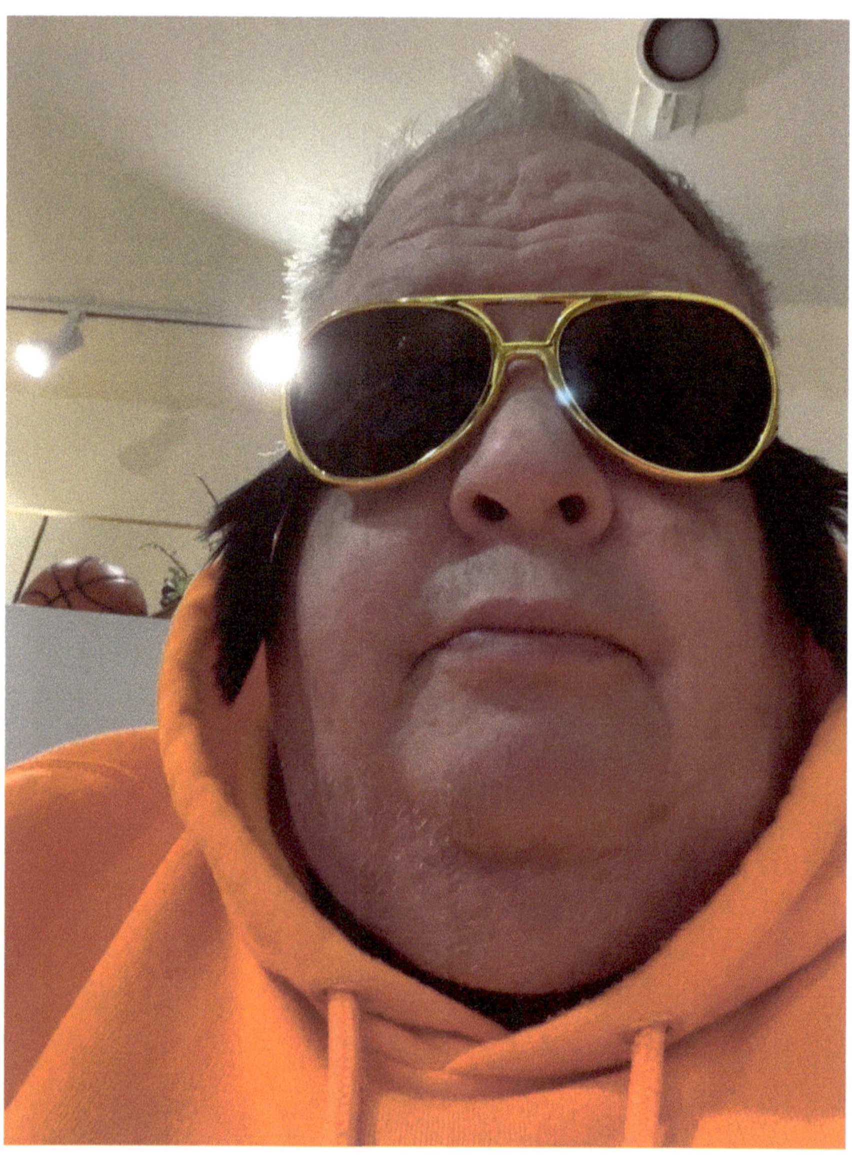

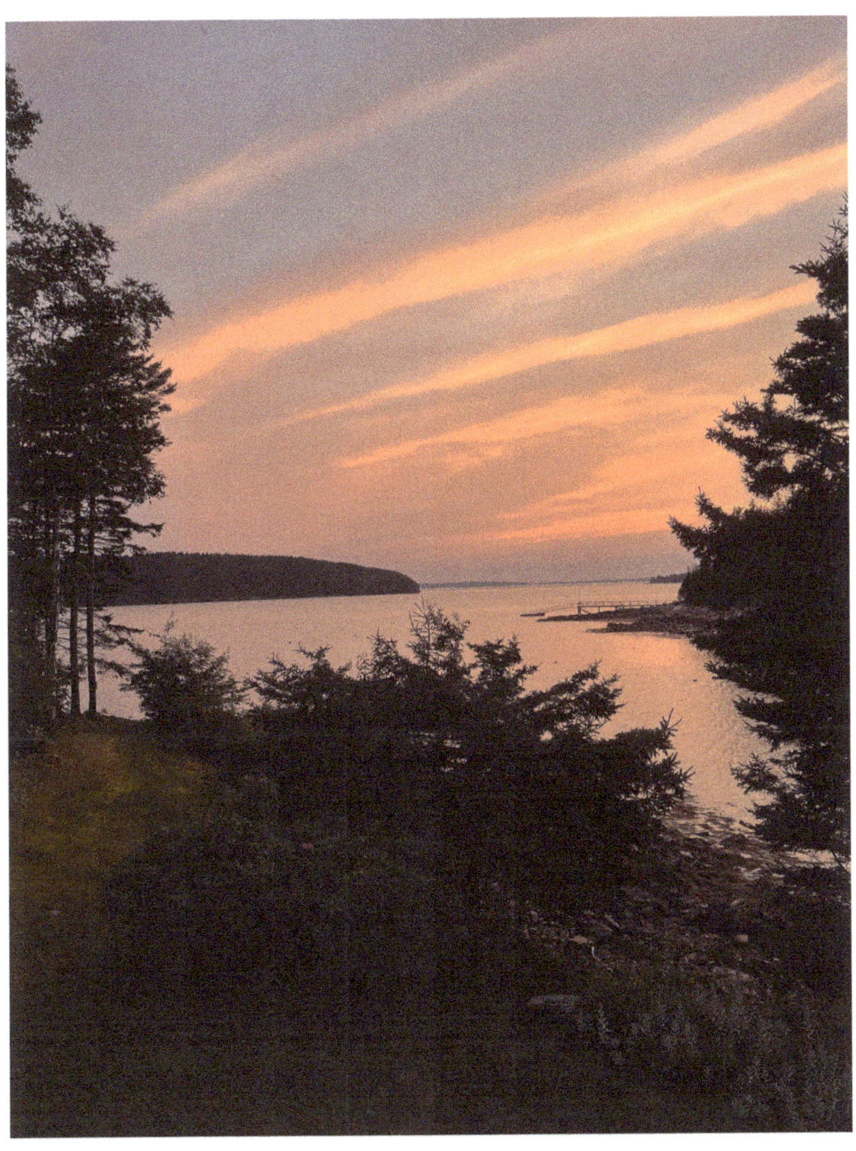

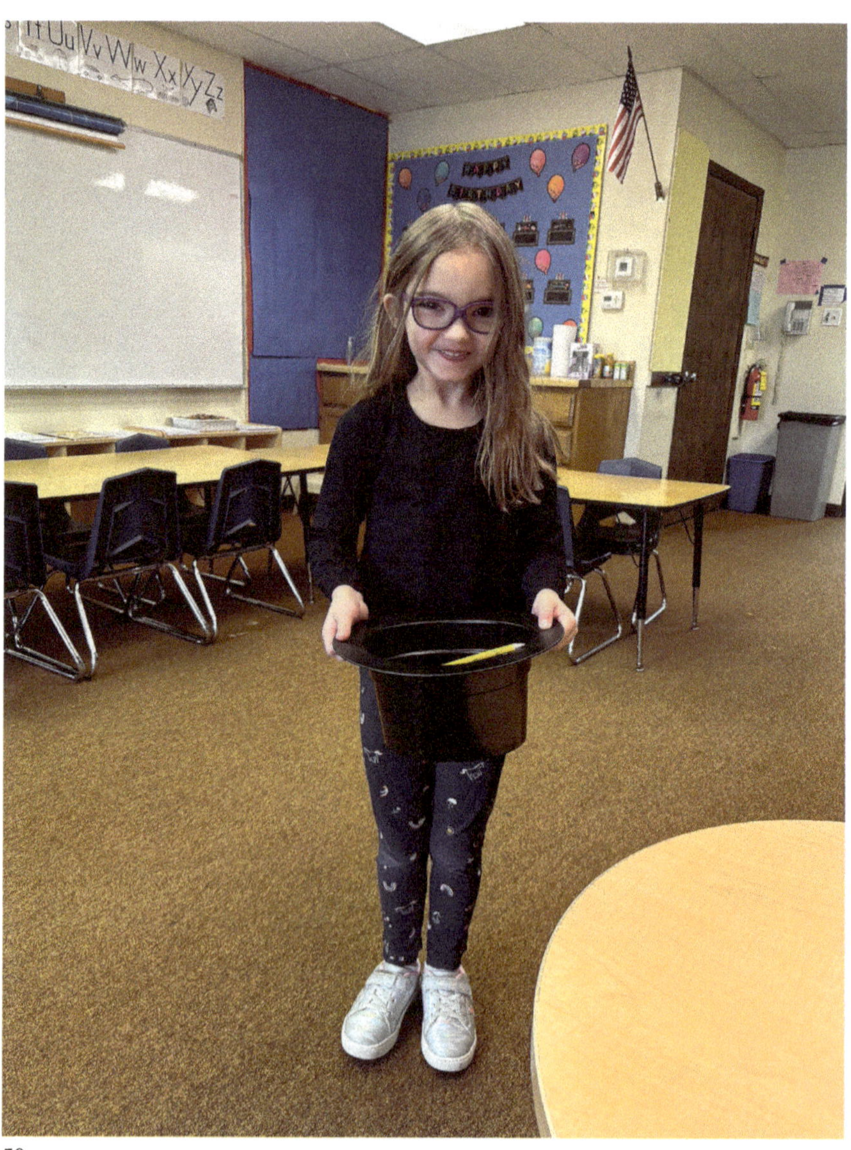

If you never had the opportunity to learn to play, get someone to teach you, without saying they need to know.

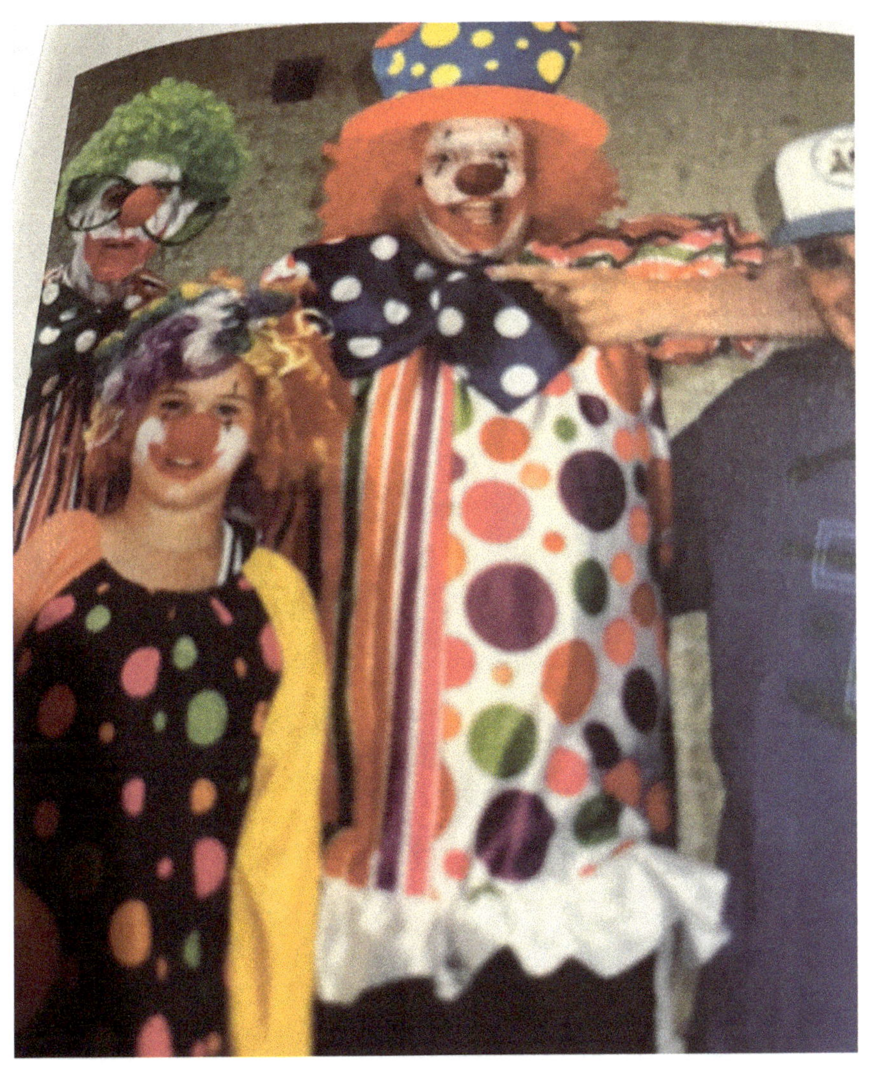

George Bernard Shaw:
"We don't stop playing because we grow old;
we grow old because we stop playing."

First tenet of care for us and for you.

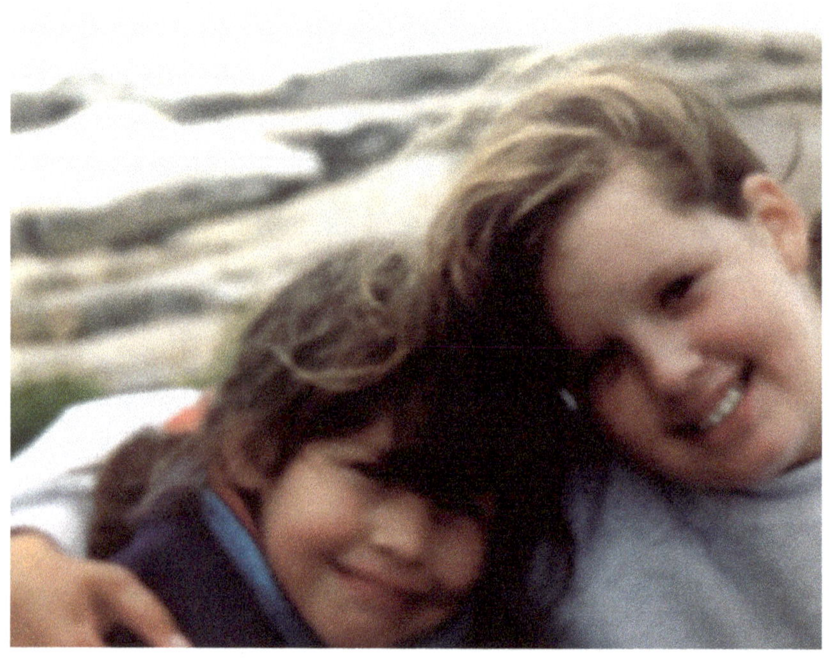

May I not be the first or last, but I'm for Obama and Liz Cheney in 2024. Two different parties fighting together to preserve democracy.

No more family holidays. Took me 6 days to recover. Dementia texting holidays.

Need a break.
Going to check out some of these birds.

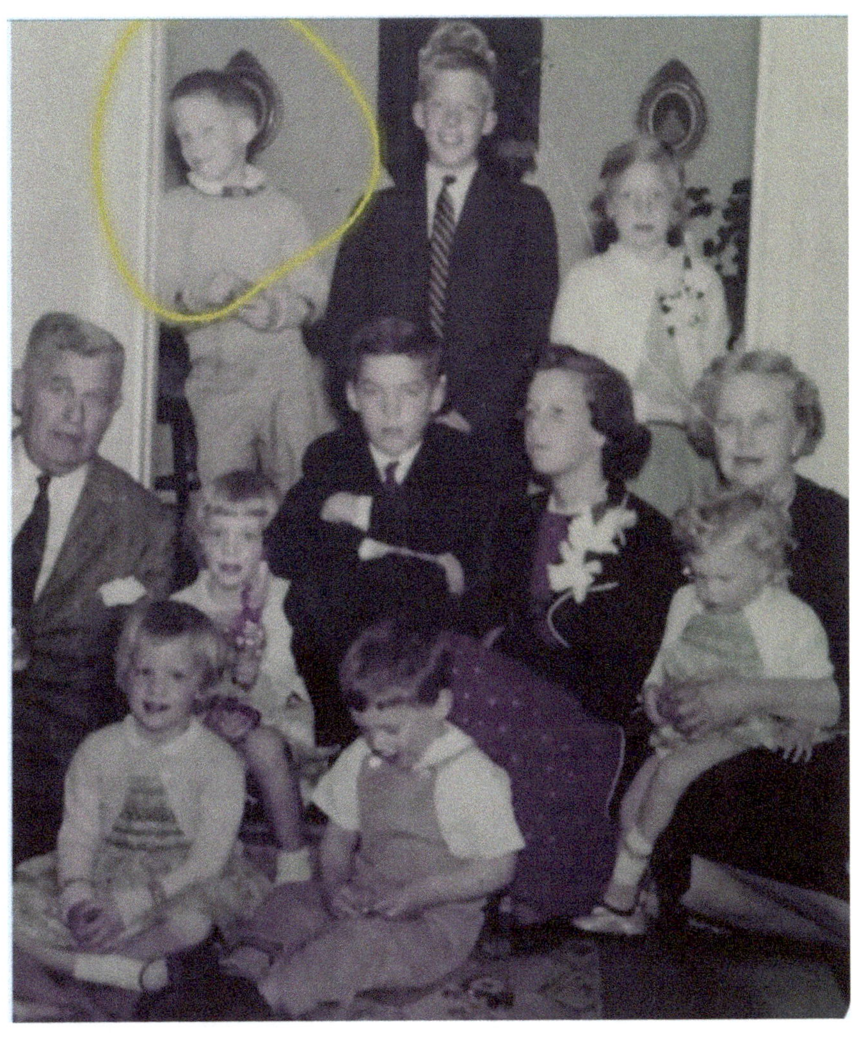

It's sorta dumb that us dementia dudes and dudettes do not like people treating us as dumb. 'Cause generally we are. I think dementia people always want to be regular. Waste-of-time dementia is fun if you try to dance with it.

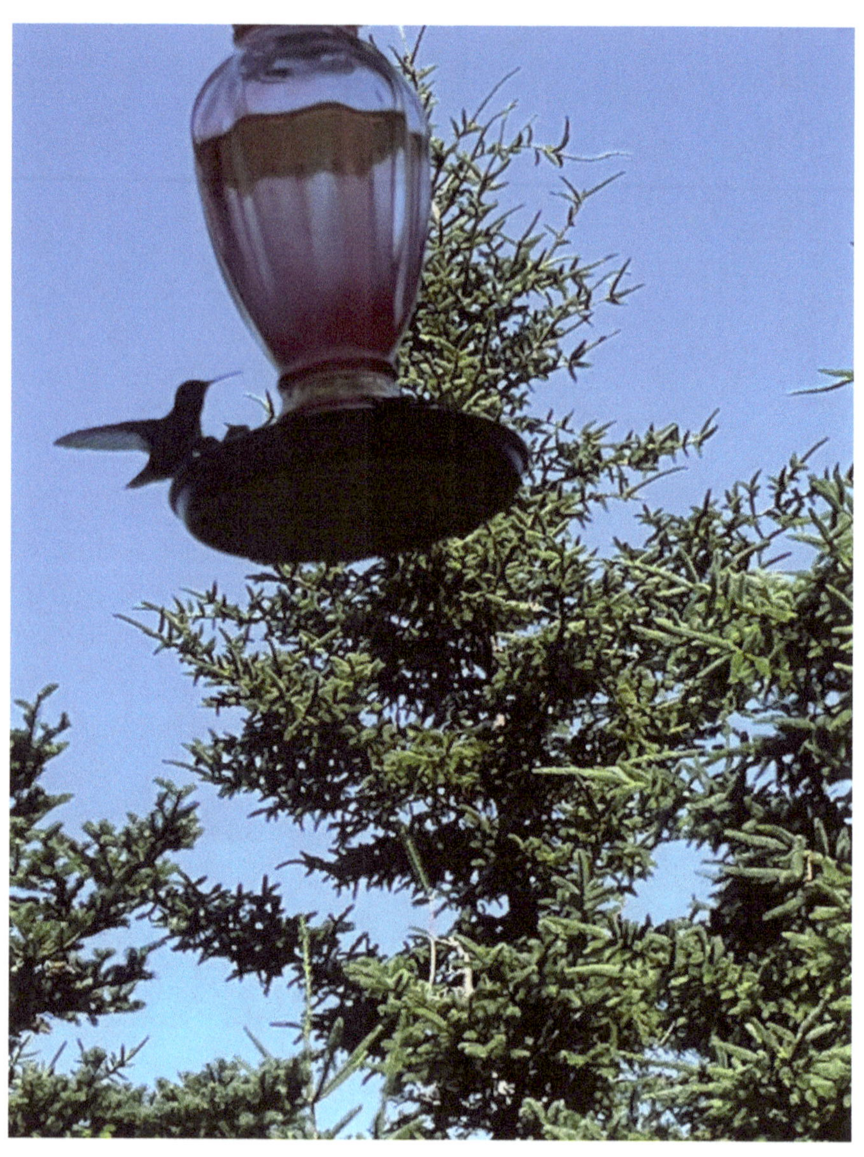

sit with It

instead of drinking It away, smoking It
away, sleeping It away, eating It away,
running from It

sit with It

you gotta feel It to heal It

I was banned with handling money for
the most part awhile back. The stove last
summer. Driving in about 1980 was out.
But this Christmas I was told I needed
help in gift giving. That's low. Oh yeah,
I can't go to the doctor's office because I
caused a little commotion…three times
before the hammer.
All good decisions by wifey.

Dementia signs different in women
vs. men.
Don't think so. The type of dementias
we have had a greater affect by far.
But the declaration applies to all of us,
everyone.

Dementiafried.

Too creepy.

The Six Types of Courage

Physical Courage: To keep going with resiliency, balance & awareness.

Social Courage: To be yourself unapologetically.

Moral Courage: Doing the right thing even when it's uncomfortable or unpopular

Emotional Courage: Feeling all your emotions (positive & negative) without guilt or attachment.

Intellectual Courage: to learn, unlearn and relearn with an open & flexible mind.

Spiritual Courage: Living with purpose & meaning through a heart centered approach towards all life and oneself.

The DAWN Method

Dementia will shuffle, reorder, and
delete our memories. But we are more
than a specific and carefully cataloged
collection of past events. We also
experience life from one moment
to the next. Shape my experiences
so they give me a sense of value and
purpose.

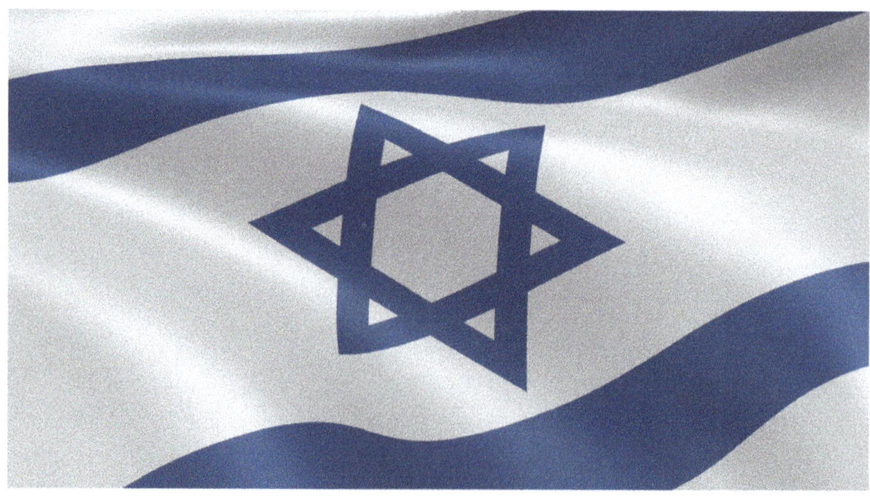

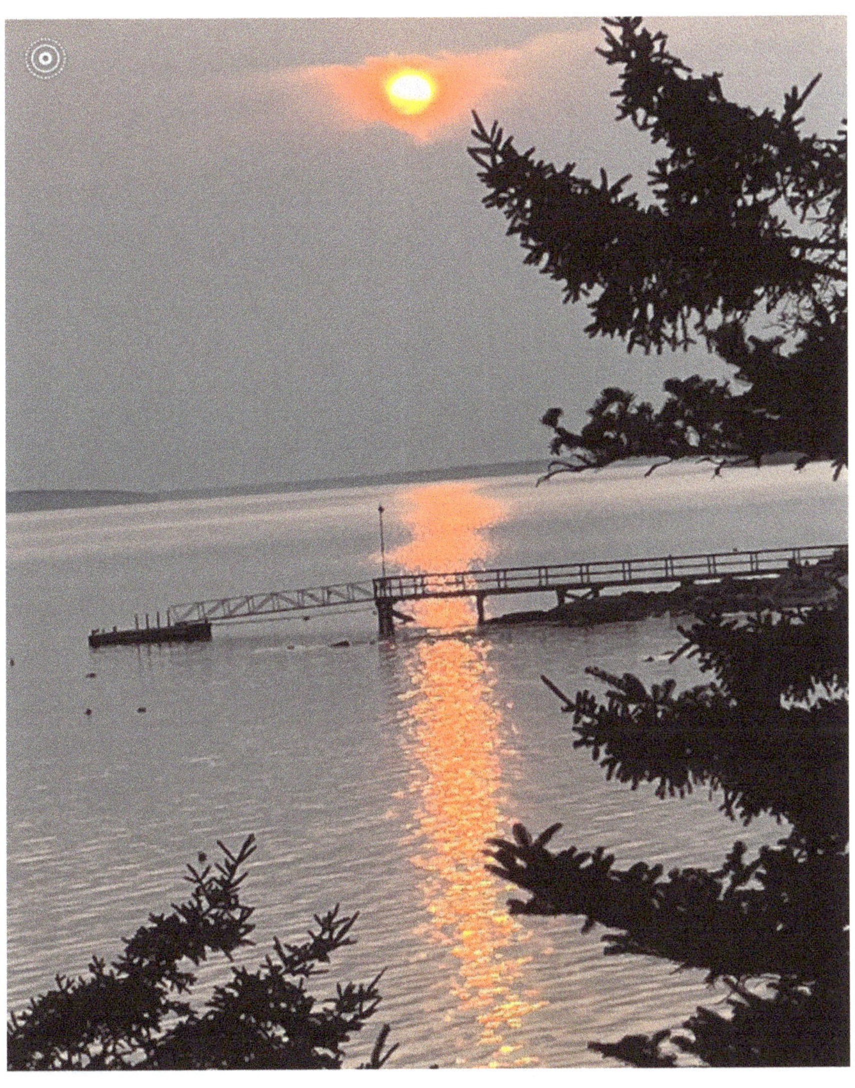

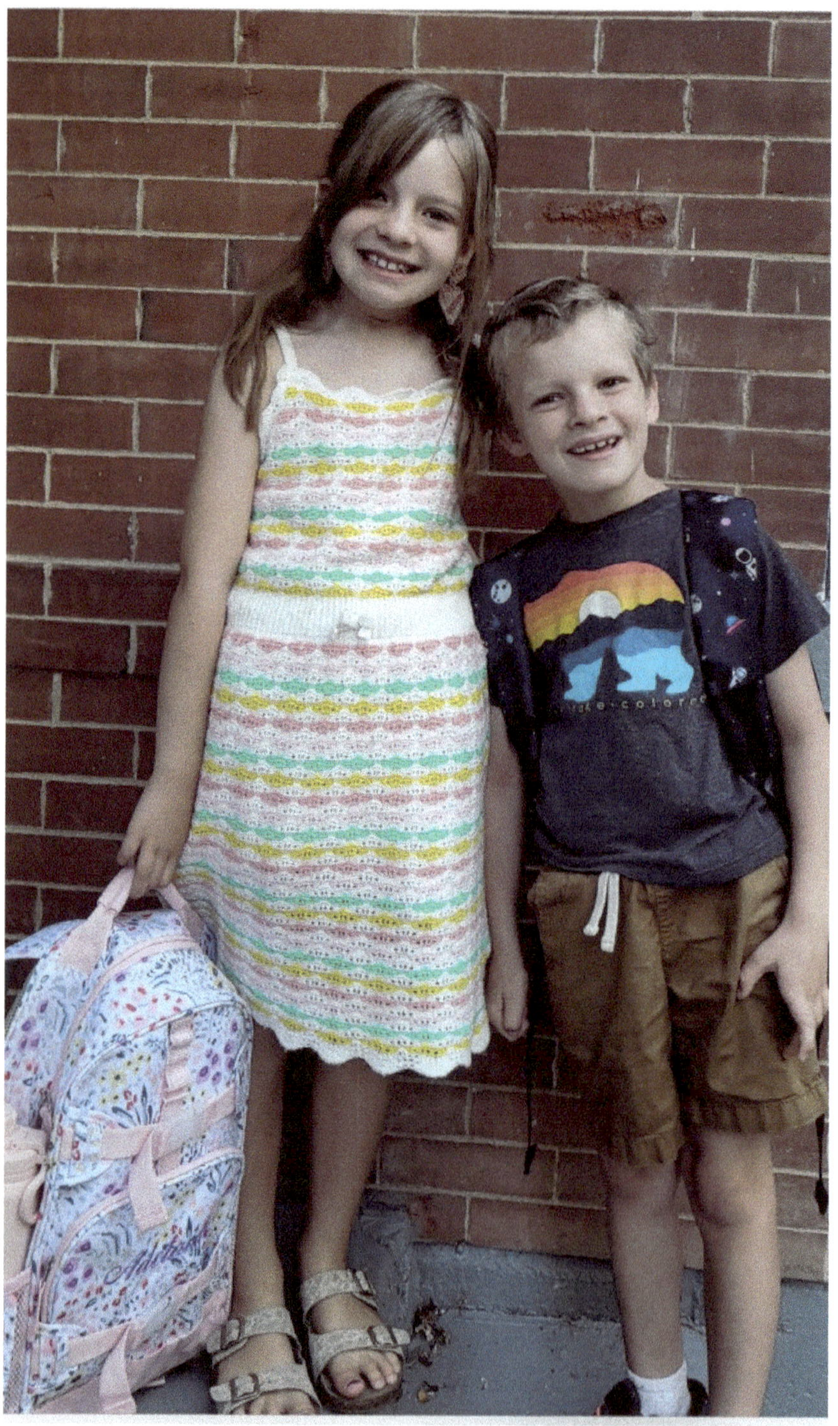

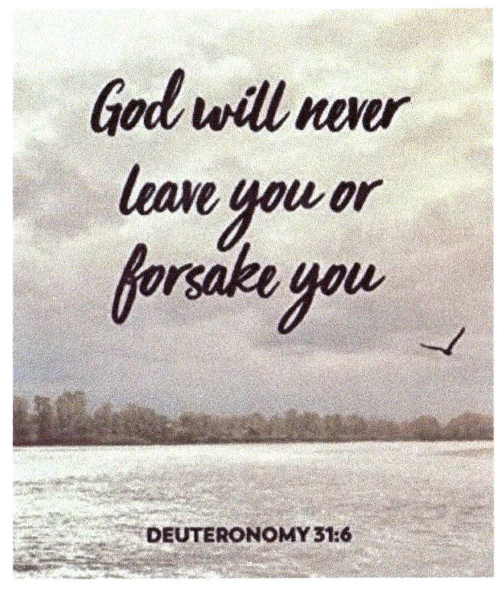

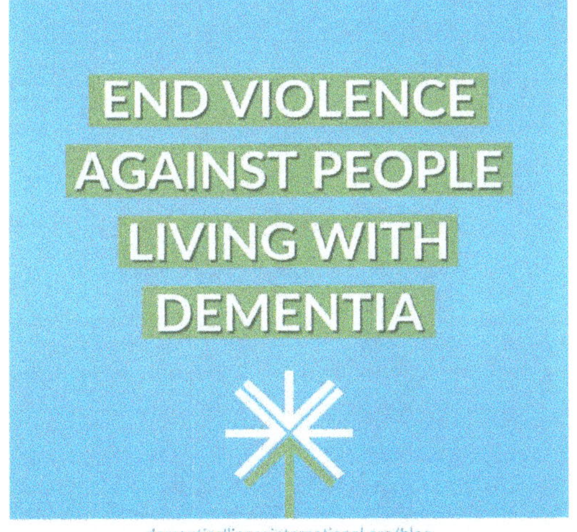
END VIOLENCE
AGAINST PEOPLE
LIVING WITH
DEMENTIA

dementiaallianceinternational.org/blog

This is My command—be strong and courageous! Do not be afraid or discouraged. For the LORD your God is with you wherever you go.

Joshua 1:9 (NLT) Read Full Chapter

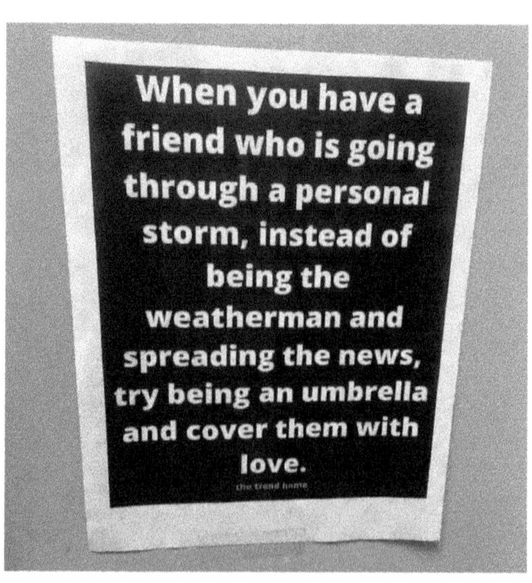

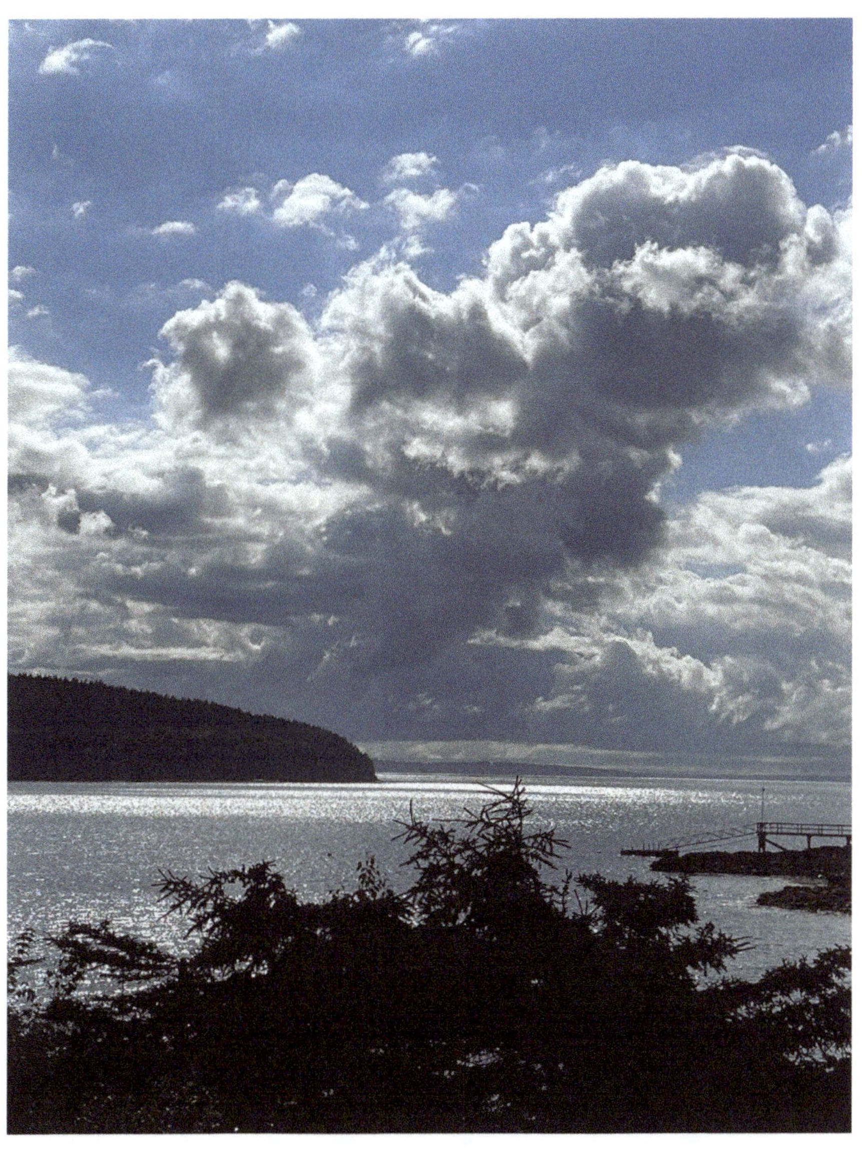

Even in the hardest times, there's still space for love, connection and purpose. And how amazing it is that YOU have the power to shape meaningful experiences and find strength in what's still possible?!

Keep going, you've got this.

Original poster: Mary Osborne

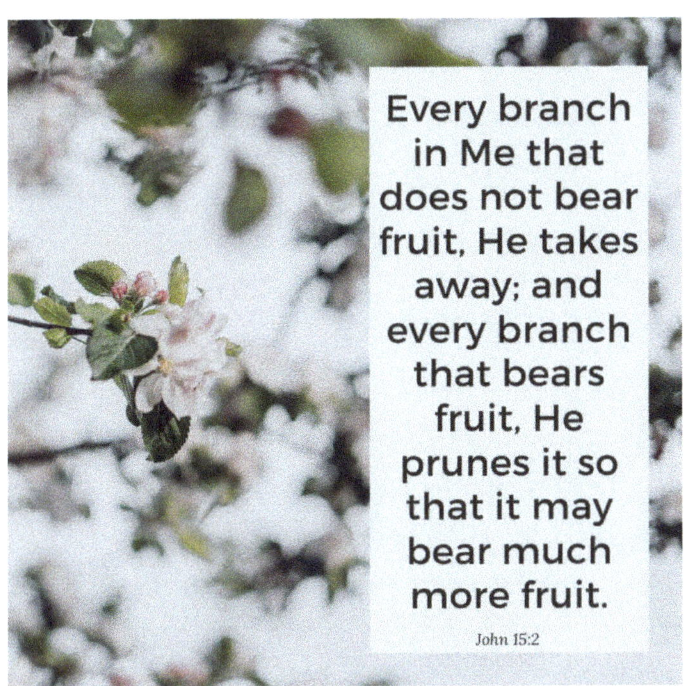

Every branch in Me that does not bear fruit, He takes away; and every branch that bears fruit, He prunes it so that it may bear much more fruit.
John 15:2

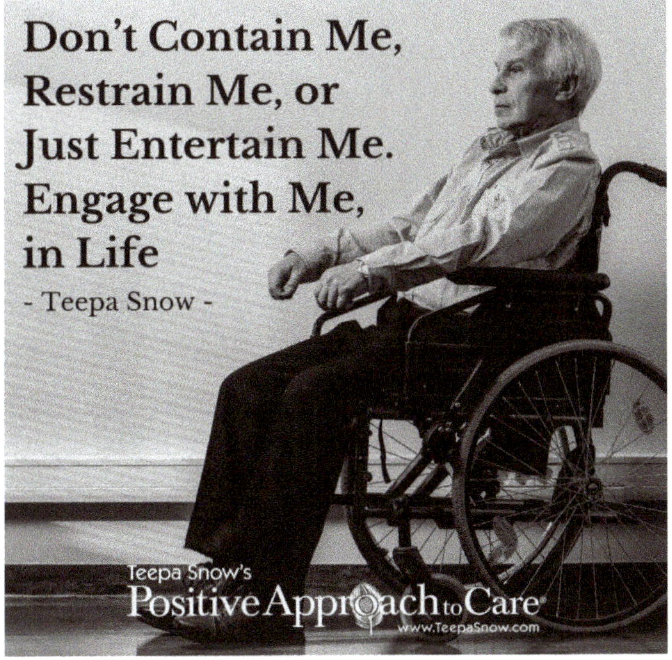

Don't Contain Me, Restrain Me, or Just Entertain Me. Engage with Me, in Life
- Teepa Snow -
Teepa Snow's
Positive Approach to Care
www.TeepaSnow.com

activist.
now • 🌐

Dementia Revolution. It seems we should demand that our regular friends and family talk to us in dementia save for brief cordial moments. 1. No Intros. 2No long stories. 3Complex sentences no.4 No interrupting us but we can interrupt regulars at any point for any reasonable reason. 5 please don't ask "if I remember".6 don't ask me about unimportant stuff x10. 7dint make me rehire my assistant who searches for filed memories. Eg. What did you do today. (My favorite)8 If multiple conversations are going on ,and that is fine, you will see me put on earphones. 9 Speak at a pace that doesn't sound like the cops chasing. Child talk and I will fake that I don't know you. 10. Be funny. Maudlin stuff and you will be escorted out. Ps if ever say I'm brave, I will say that y feet stink.

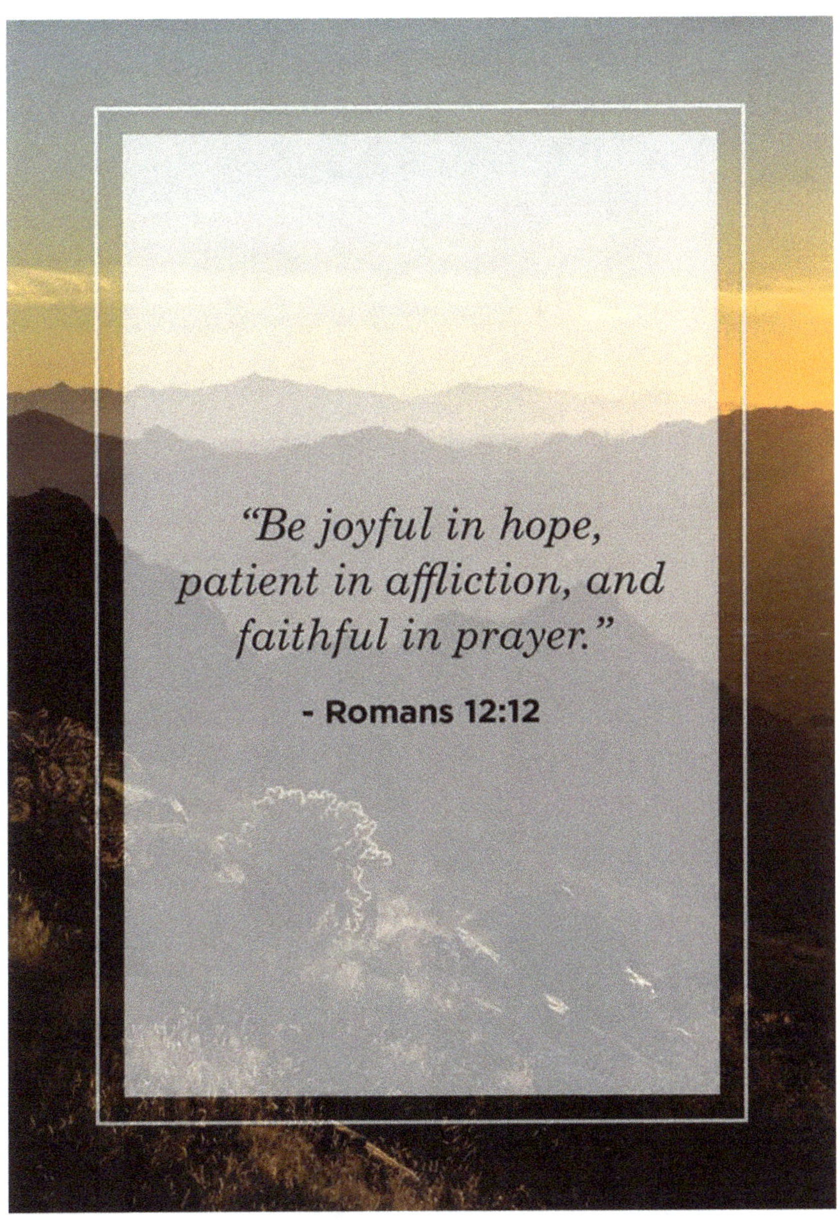

"Be joyful in hope, patient in affliction, and faithful in prayer."
- Romans 12:12

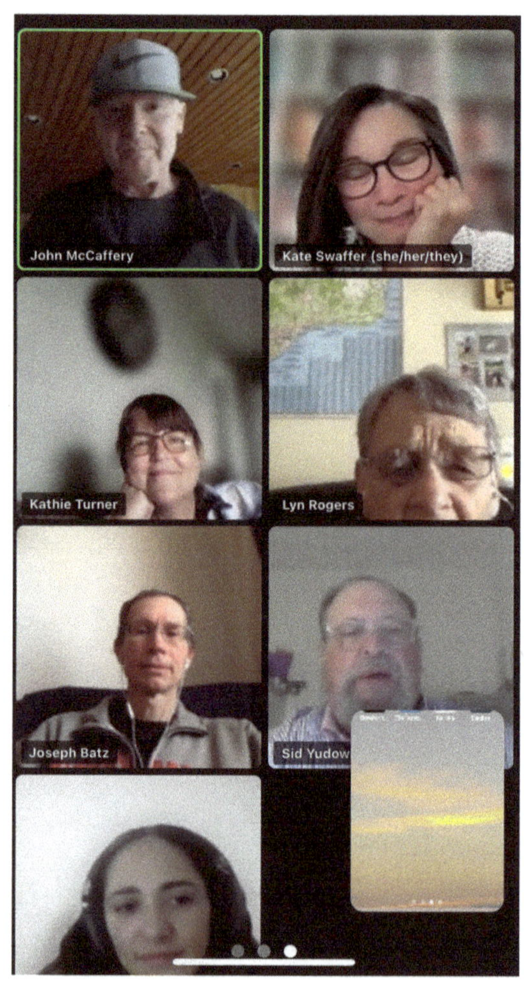

Some Zoomer friends

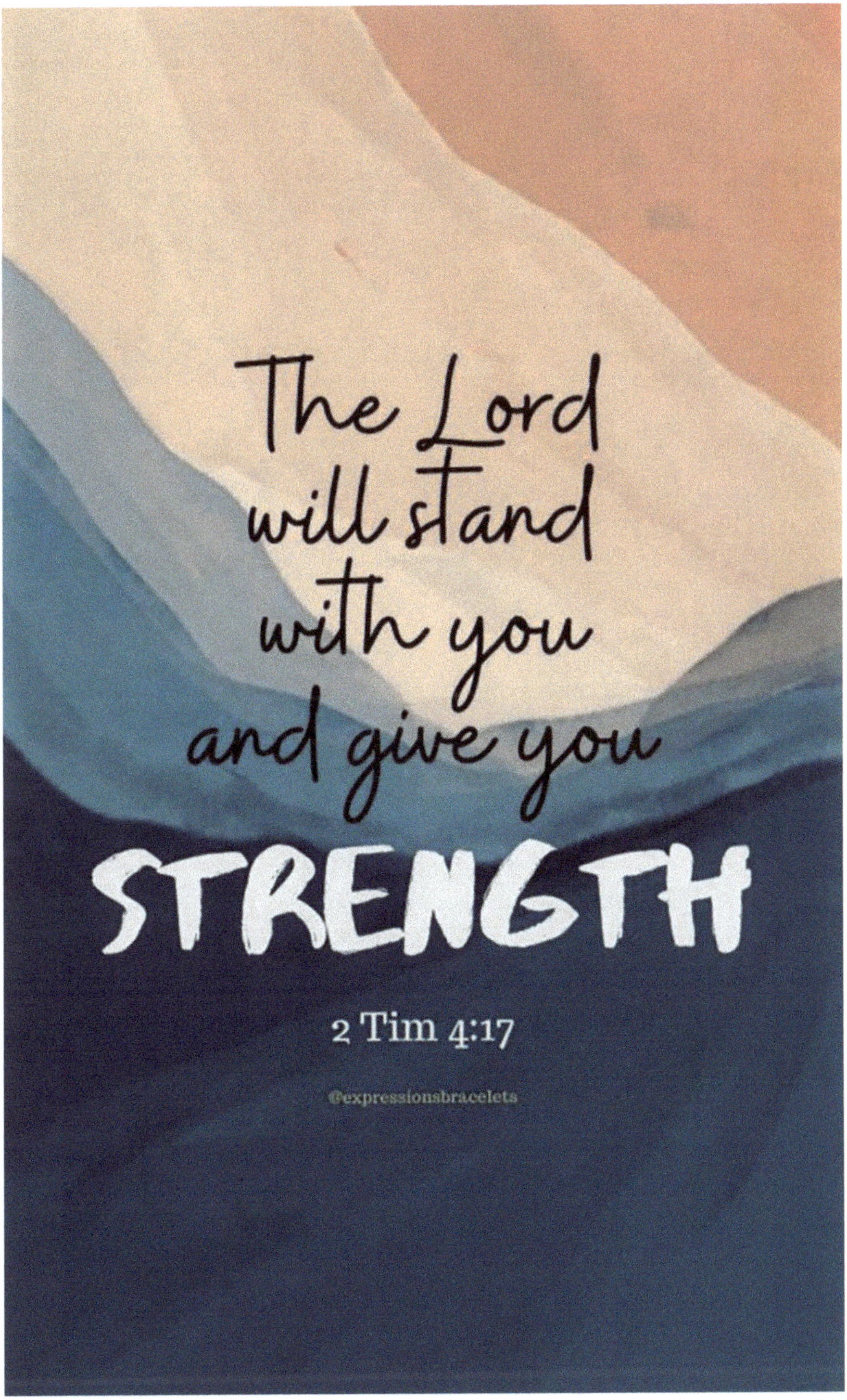

The Lord
will stand
with you
and give you
STRENGTH
2 Tim 4:17
@expressionsbracelets

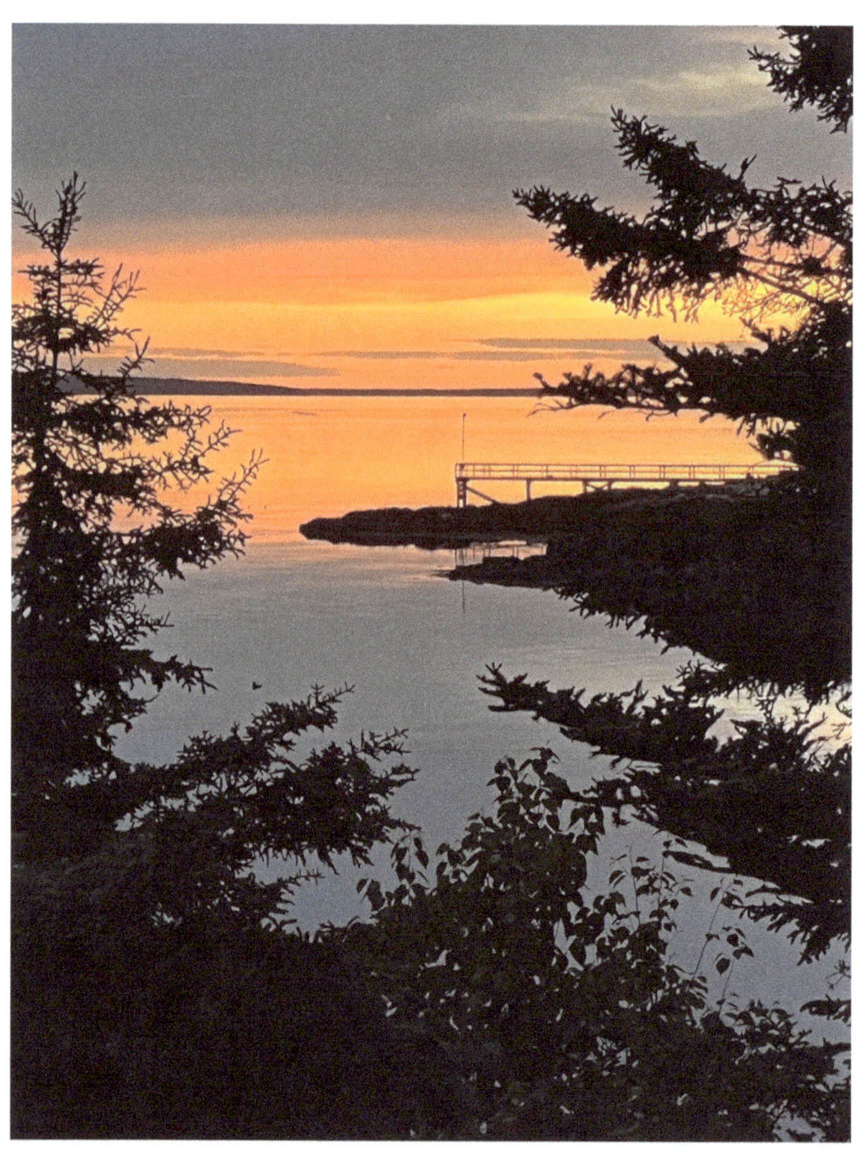

7:14

← •••

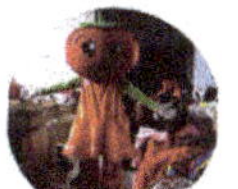 **Dallas Dixon** • You
Dementia author and wanna be
dementia advocate and activist.
now • 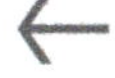

I'm embarrassed to say that I really
like being alone. It's not a
psychological component o f
dementia.Its part not having to play
with regulars.its part where I like to be
and certainly doing non cognitive
things as I use the low battery flicker.
❤️ 👍🏽 🙏🏽

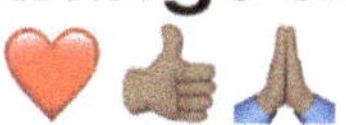 👍 Like   💬 Comment

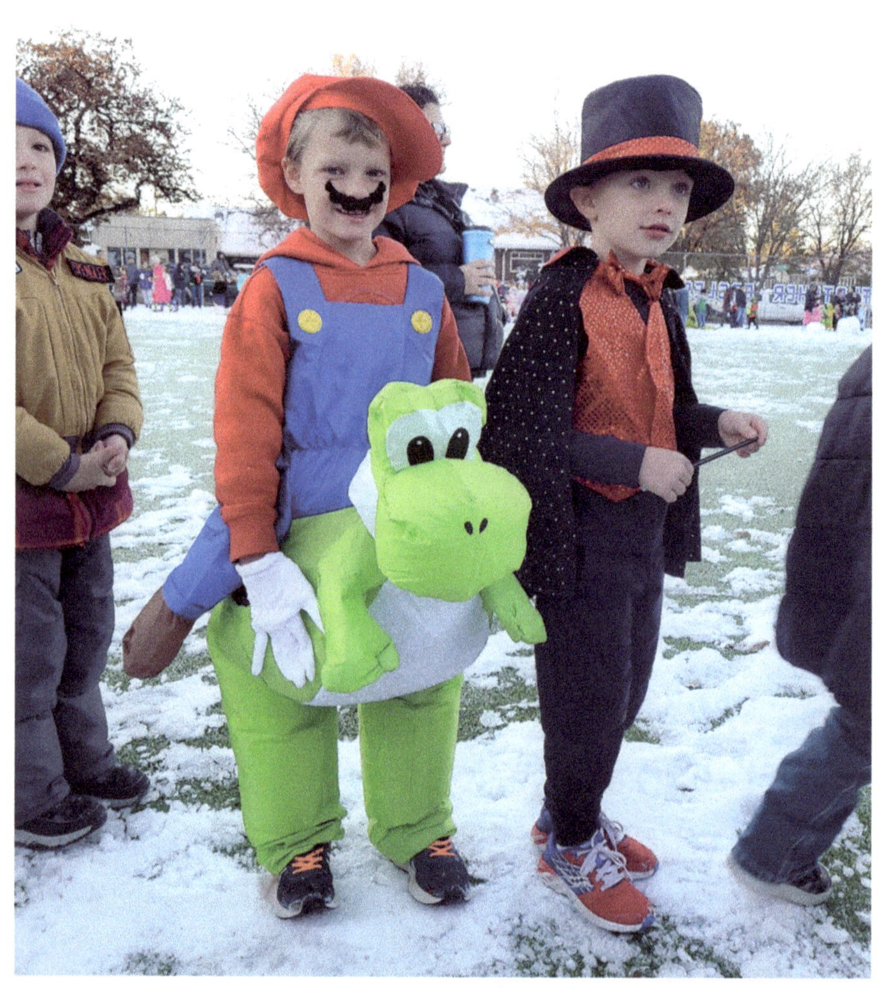

God knows my name…
even if I don't know yours or mine..

So I never really bought the idea
of dementia folks mourning
before their time.

And I never understood why
many of us worry about spouses
cheating post-diagnosis.

Some is basic. Mourning by
squeezing too hard and the
breathless threat of us becoming
worthless is present.

A mourning at diagnosis.

Dementia helps me to notice

the Beauty, Majesty

and Love of God

everywhere

and in everything.

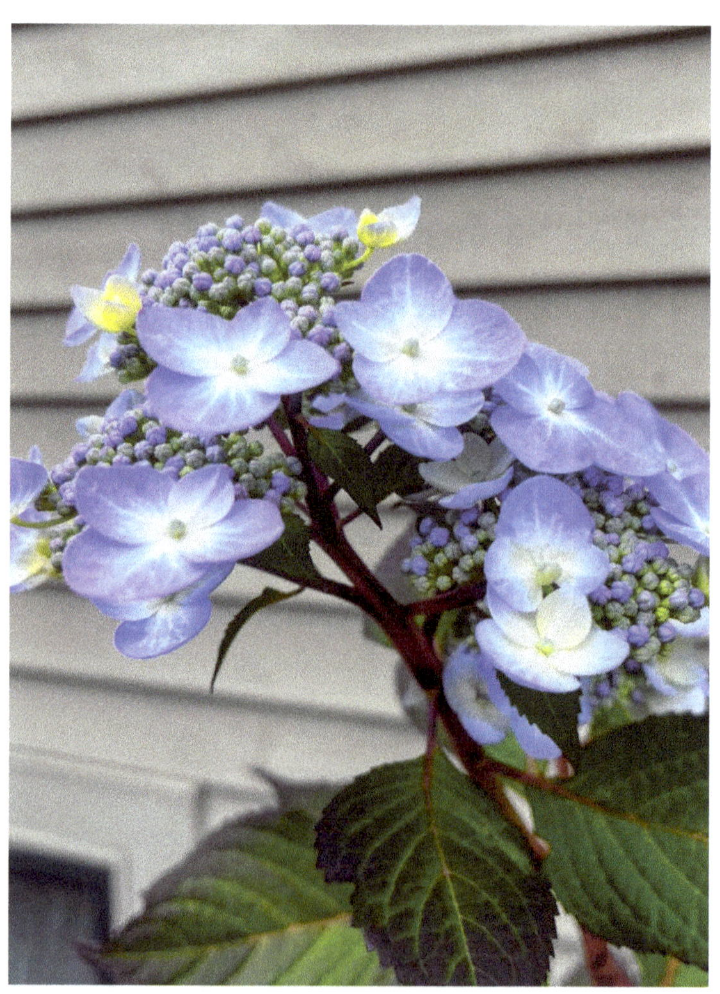

74

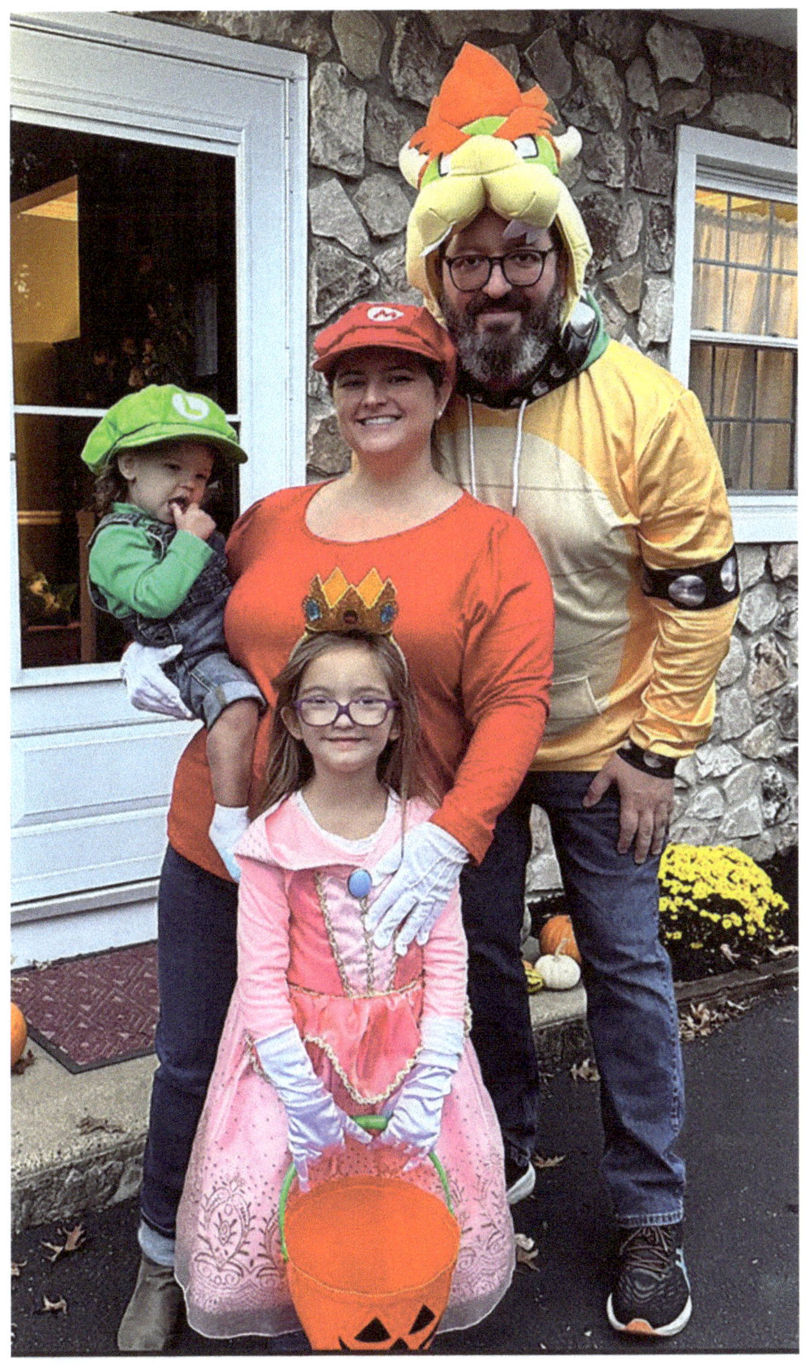

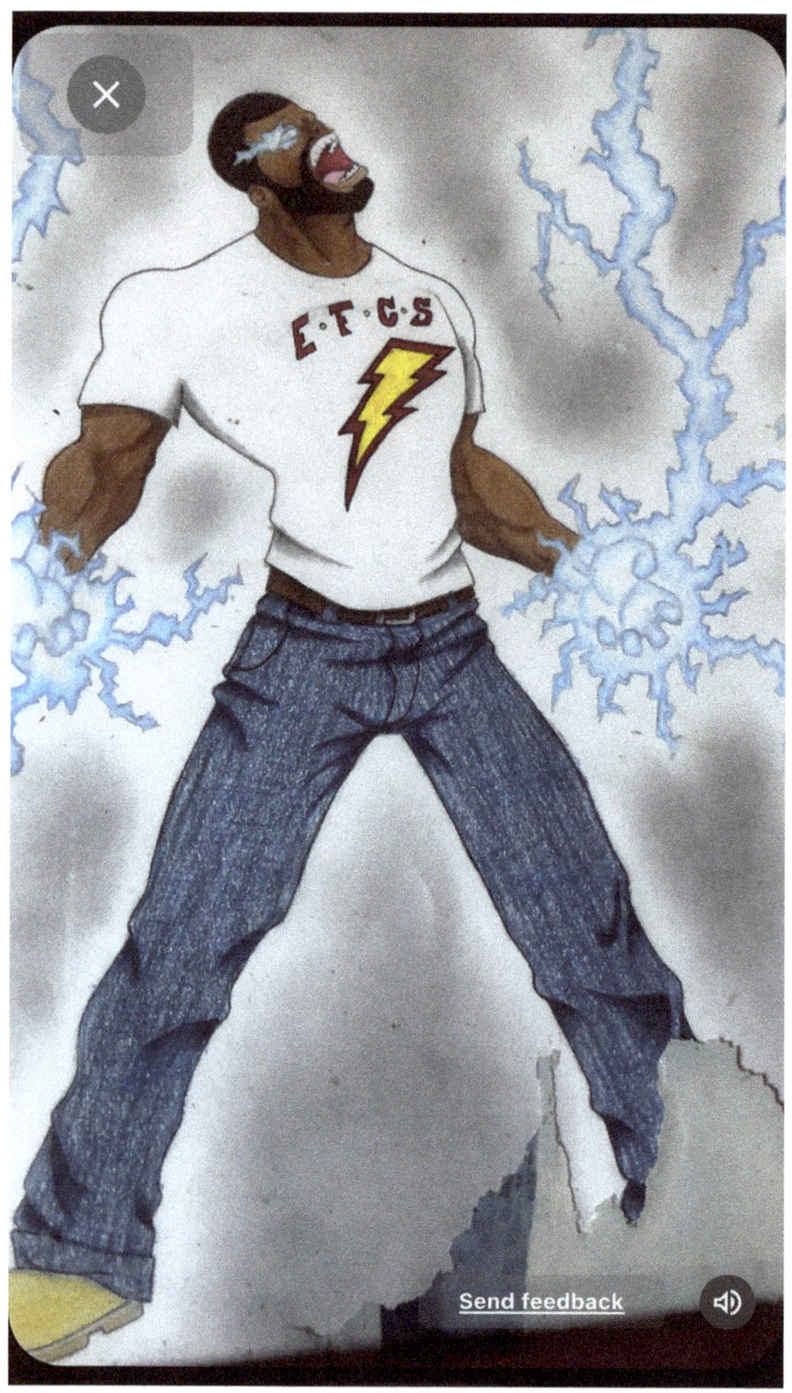
E·T·C·S
Send feedback

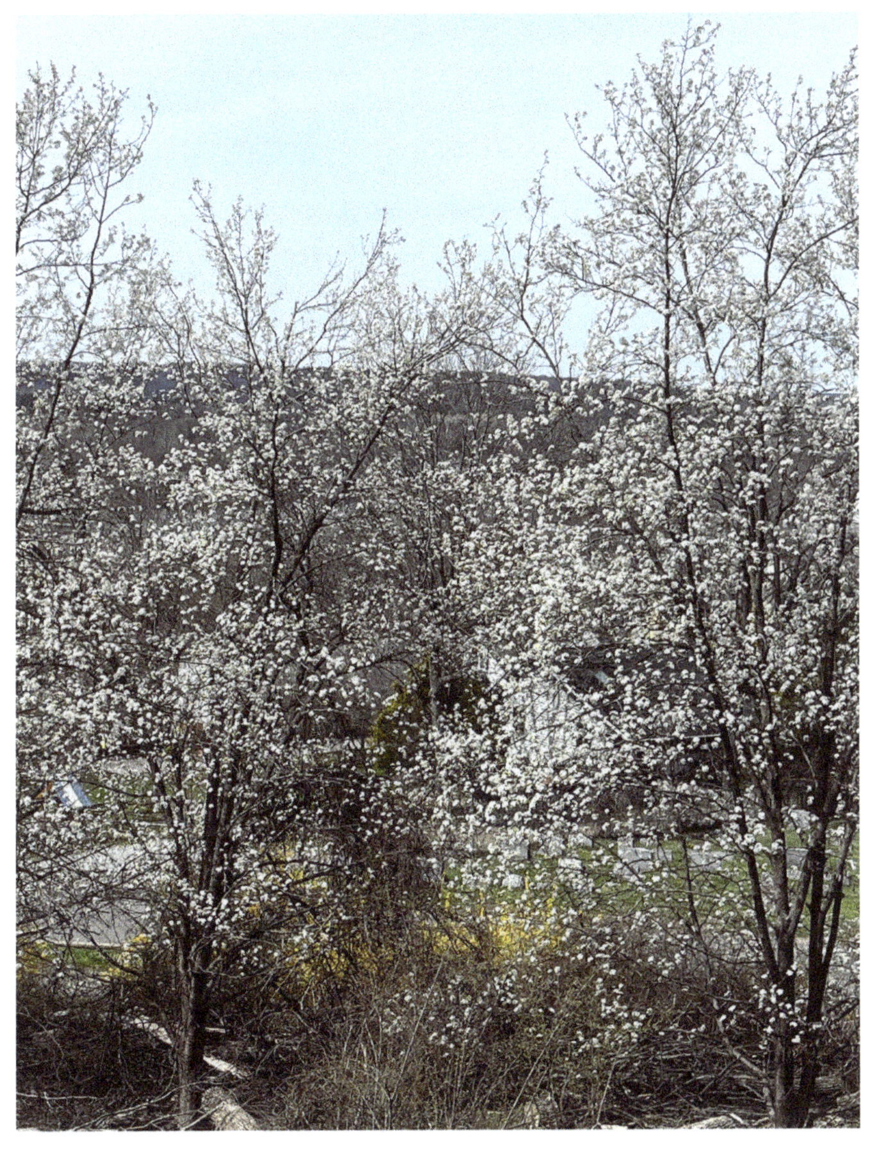

Caregiving can take the fun out of dementia.

Plus I will never take more than 1$ for it.

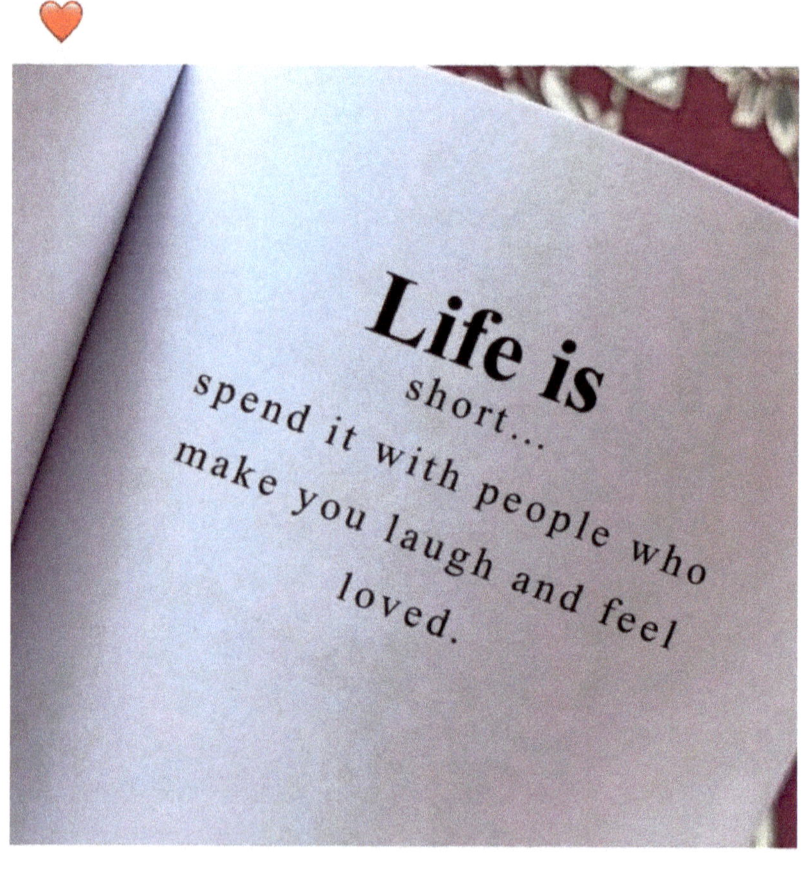

Life is
short...
spend it with people who
make you laugh and feel
loved.

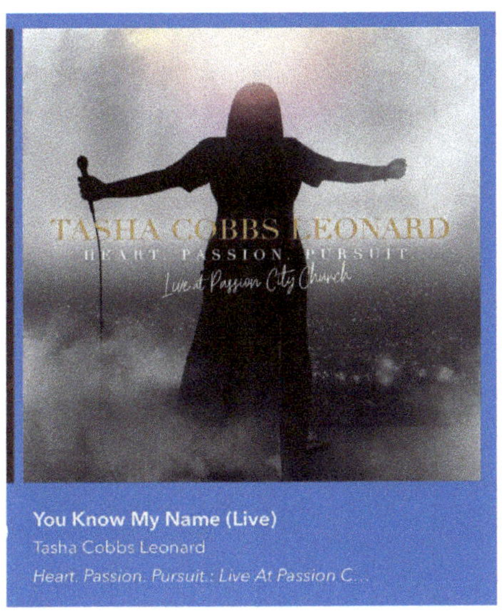

I'm encouraged to see more people speaking up about their dementia and actively shifting the stigma.
Not long ago, I came across a few wonderful support groups designed specifically for people with dementia.
Support groups offer an important way to meet the emotional, social, and mental needs of individuals living with dementia.
These spaces allow people to connect with others who truly understand their experiences, helping to reduce feelings of isolation.
They provide an opportunity for individuals to share their stories, draw inspiration from others, and build a sense of community & belonging. . .
all essential elements of a fulfilling life,
even as cognitive changes progress.
These programs are truly inspiring! Some focus on social opportunities, while others take a more traditional support group approach.
Laura Herman

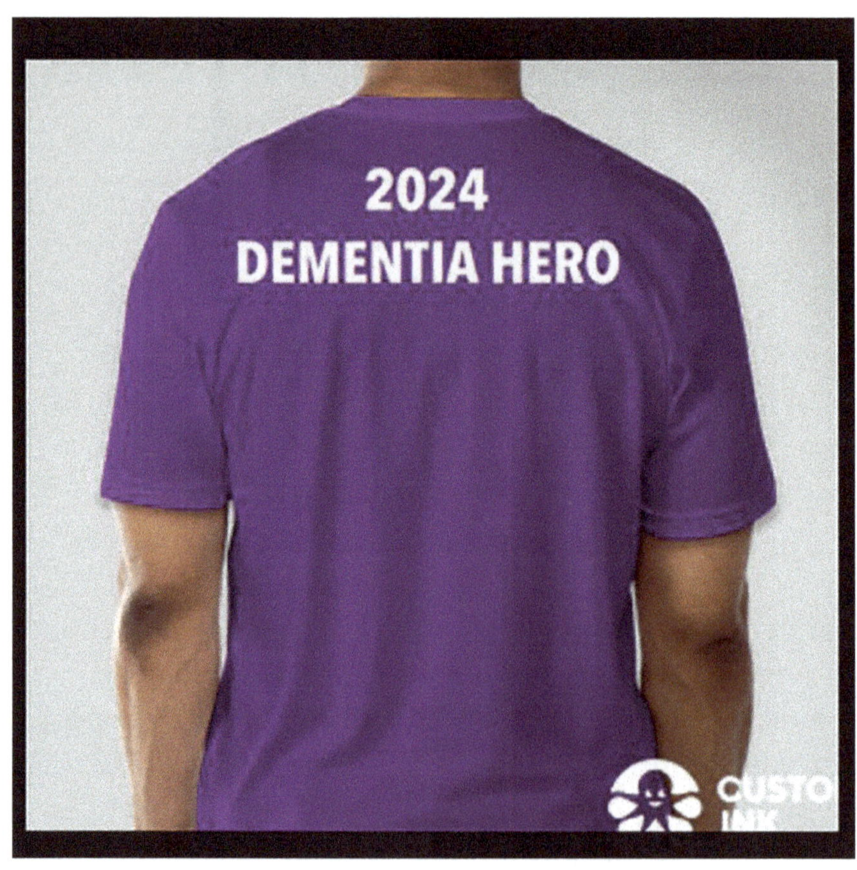

Death and dementia are not the same.

Don't blame us for death.

That's over our pay grade.

PS. I no longer accept fear in my soul.

The Dementia Dog…a Superhero for every Dementia Dude and Dudette and every organization.

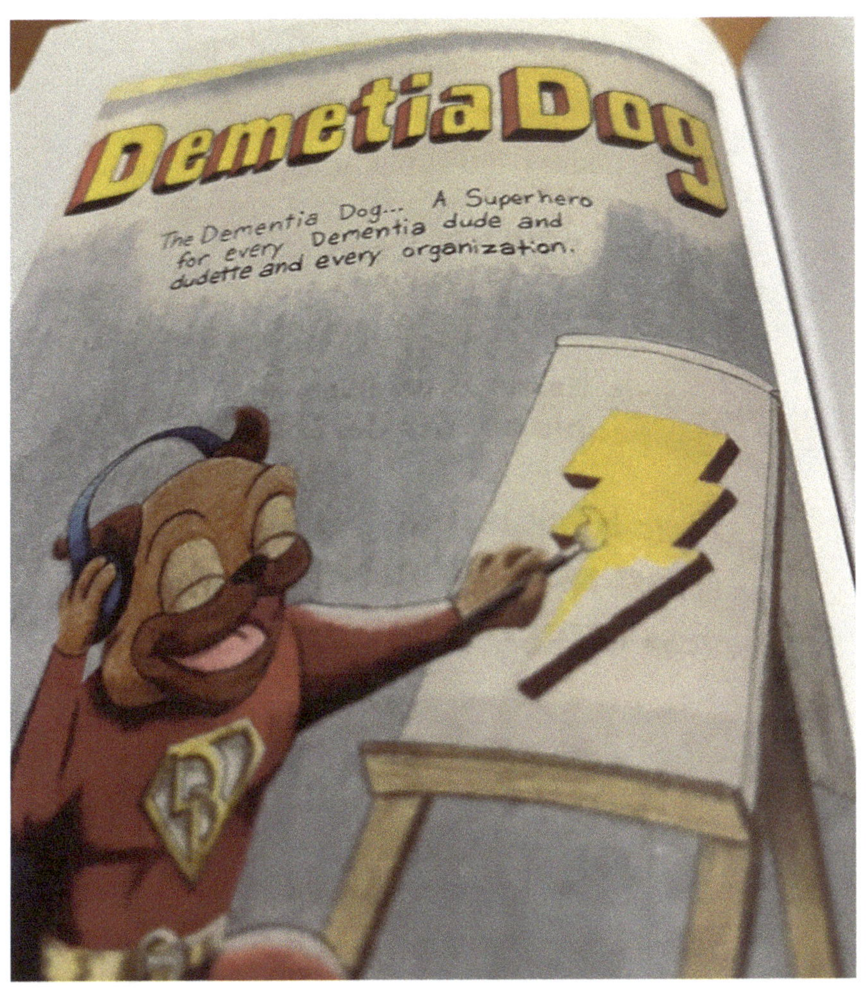

DementiaDog
The Dementia Dog... A Superhero for every Dementia dude and dudette and every organization.

What thoughts?

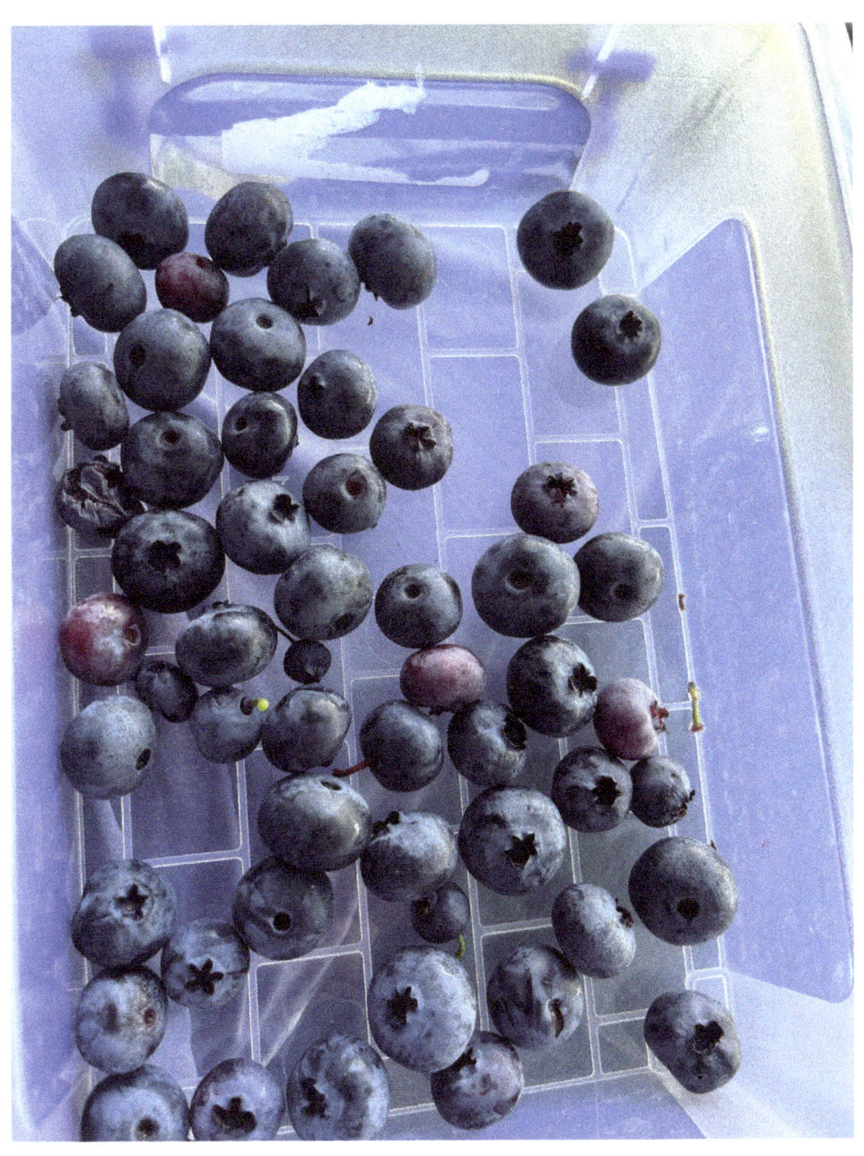

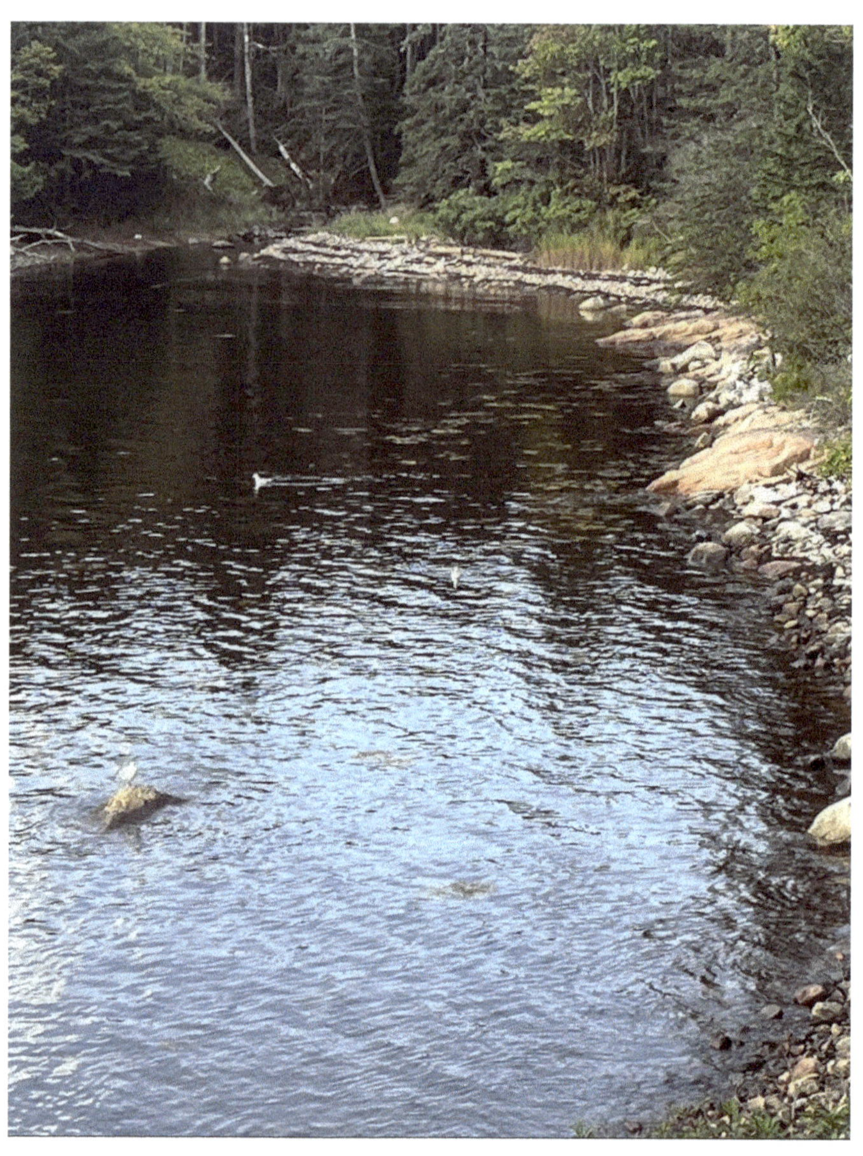

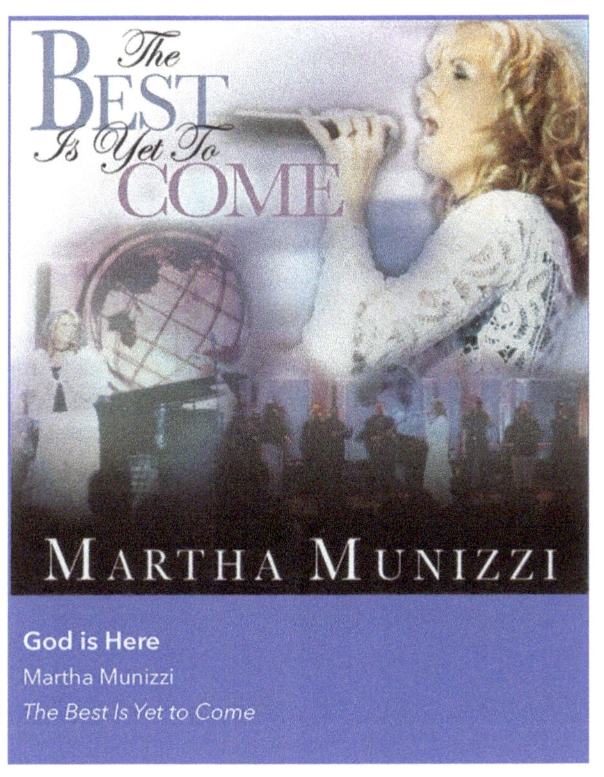

"There are only four kinds of people in the world: those who have been caregivers, those who are currently caregivers, those who will be caregivers, and those who will need caregivers."

—Rosalyn Carter

Best Quotes of the Day
1,322,661 followers
13m
Stop using your energy to worry.
Use your energy to believe, create, love, grow, glow, manifest, and heal.

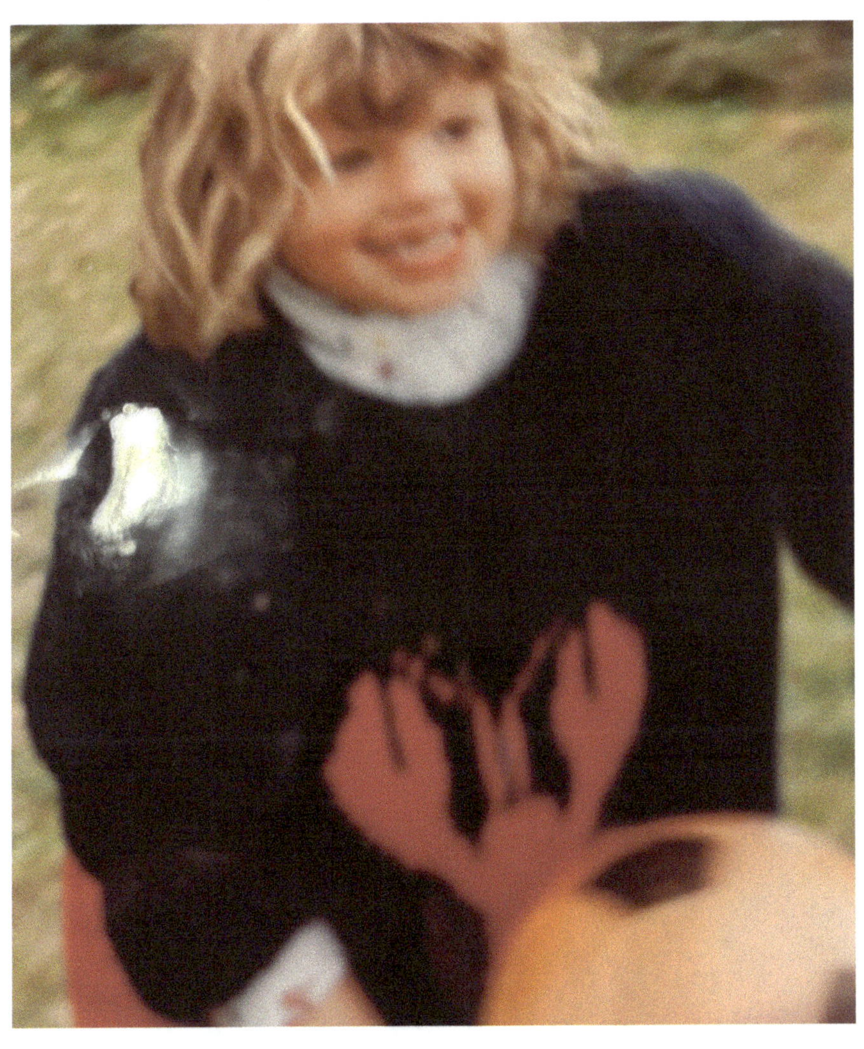

I am the best dementia teacher

in the whole world...

along with hundreds of other dementia dudes and

dudettes.

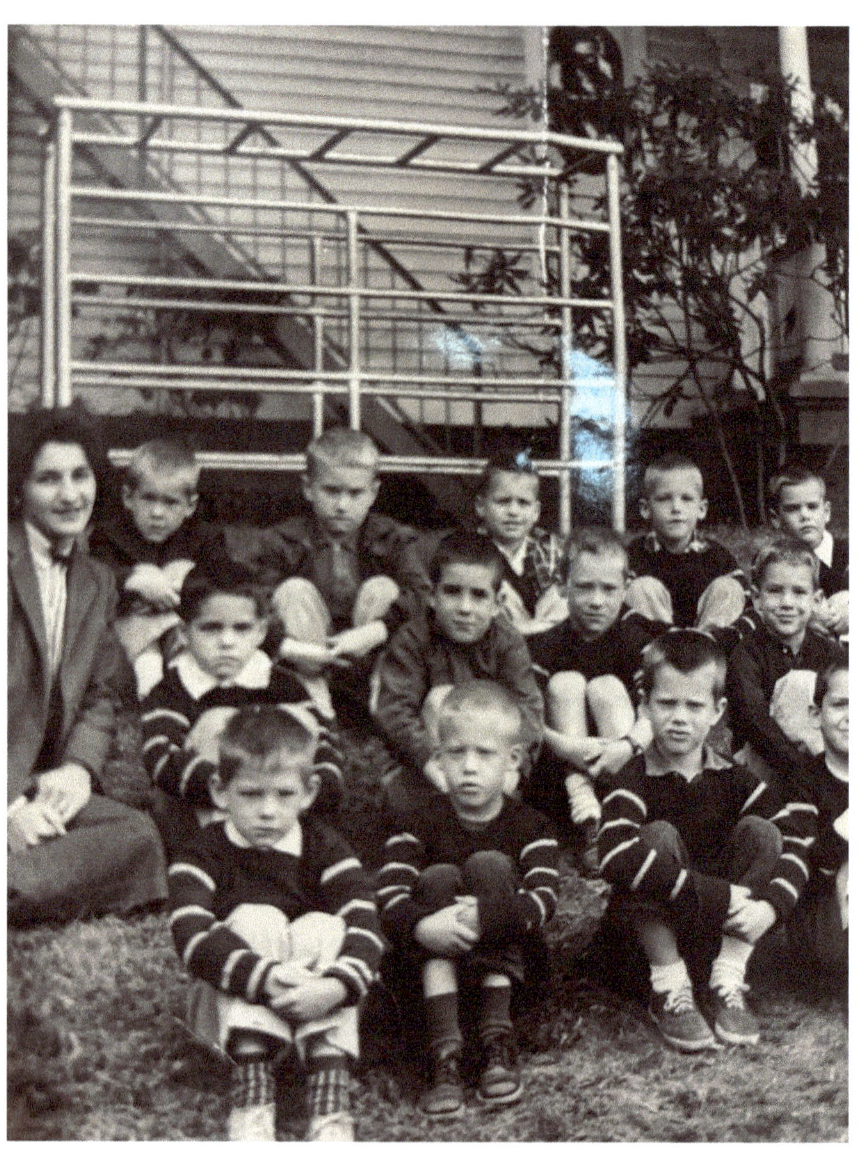

I never forget but I lie like a dog.

Teaching on processing delay.

Dementia and Joy perfect together.

Harry, where art u?

Scripture. 1 Corinthians 13:4–8a (ESV) Love is patient and kind; love does not envy or boast; it is not arrogant or rude. It does not insist on its own way; it is not irritable or resentful; it does not rejoice at wrongdoing, but rejoices with the truth.

Love resists
Envy (isn't envi
Boasting (isn't t
Arrogance (isn't
Rudeness (isn't
Selfishness (doe
Anger (isn't irrit
Resentment (isr
Wrongdoing (d

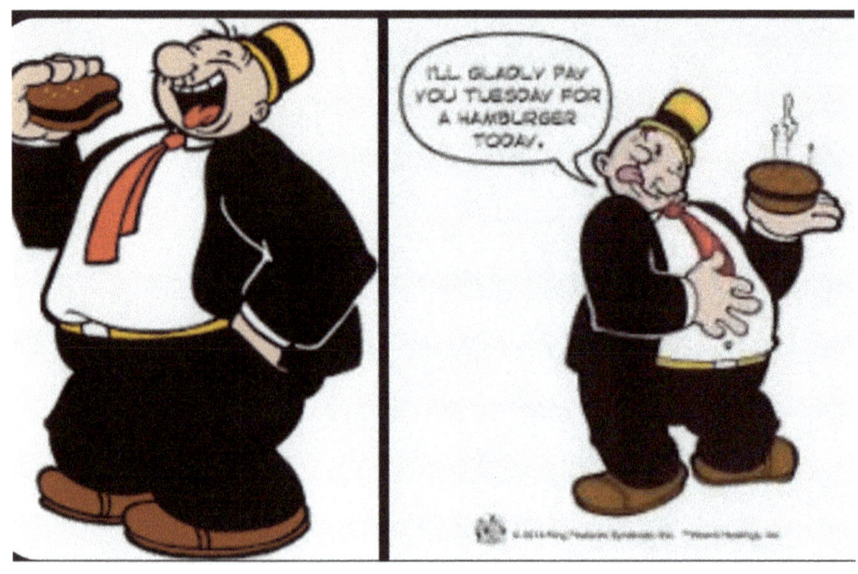

Blah blah.

There are great new terms, but back in my day,
I discovered the word "fronting." Which means
pretending you're someone you're not. We do that.
We dementia people pretend to be regulars, even for
a moment. Dangerous territory. My moments never
turned out well. Sometimes we are conscious of our
choice, sometimes not. Either way, remember how
tiring it is to fake it. Especially for us. Trust me on this.

Do not feel sorry for us dementia people. It doesn't help
us and doesn't help you.

Fun and joy is the new dementia goal. In whatever "stage" we are in, this is it.

I respectfully suggest that to emphasize the worst is counterproductive at best. We should be inventing times of joy not torture. If teepa, teepa is wrong. Where are the dementia people input? Most wrong post I've seen in years.

BOYCOTT Alzheimer's Association.

The heavens proclaim the glory of God. The skies display His craftsmanship.

Psalm 19:1 (NLT) Read Full Chapter

Dementia Heroes 2024
p.2

Prince Ptah-Hotep
Augueste Deiter   Patrick Ettenes
Margaret Lock   Oliver James
Rosaln Carter   Belinda Mason
Vicky Fitch   BreAnna Wilson
Bob Murray   Jessica Cannon
Rose Ong   Michelle Olson
Sally Fauth   William Yates
"anyone who has dementia" James Vickers
Bobby Hodgin-Taylor   Debra Bein
Ashley Steven   Erinne Stewart
Mark Bletsoe   Richard + Lisa
Rufus   Debbie Saltsavage
Gertrude Jordan   PAGE 2   Sonia
Kathie Norris   Michelle Harris
Jngulyn Revere   DEMENTIA   Alister Robinson
Ichu Swinton   HEROES   Bill Yates
Sid Xudowrtch   2024   Trish Bowen
Barbara Prud'hommaux   Jaguline Wong
Alma Valencia   Gary Johnson
Rick Nalle   Linda Brewster
Bob Murray   Janine Whited
Paul Lea   Lyn Rogers
Rachel Wonderlin   John McCaffery
Ann Sutter   Karen Stobbe
Niacie P. Smith   Lori LeBey
                            Mike Belleville
Steve's Mom

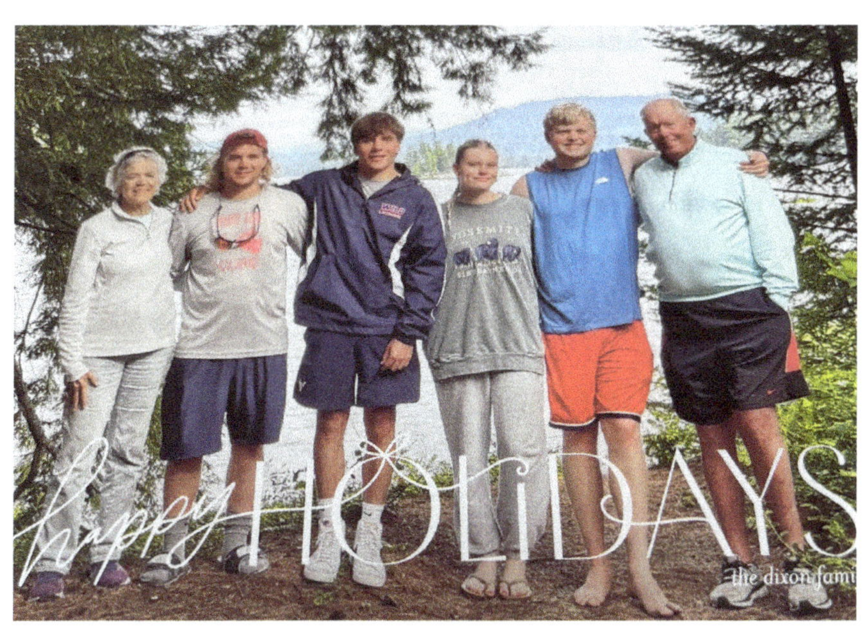

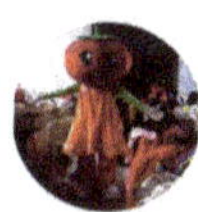

Dallas Dixon • You
Dementia author and wanna be
dementia advocate and activist.
now •

Have you aver had a brilliant
moment.Then while you are busy
patting yourself on the on the back ,
you remember thadementia or not you
are not smart enough for it to be your
moment. U actually tried to cheat God
out of his mercy And Grace. And sstill
loves us so much that he actually
gave up his Boy. Merry Christmas

Dementia Heroes
2024 ~~page 3~~

Donna Marentay
Judy Cornish
Jerry Wylie
Maria Turner
Sira Botes
Craig Colligan
Roger Marple
Wally Cox
Pat Summit

EB White
Bobby Redman

Cheryl Day :
Dr Ting Fei Ho
Dr. Richard Taylor
Curry Whisenhunt
Linda Szypula
Dr. Md Nurul Hode
Eddie Albert
Sugar Ray Robinson
Norman Rockwell
Graeme Atkins
Jacqui Bingham
Perry Como
Robin Williams
Sean Connery
Ronald Reagan
Charles Bronson
Rita Hayworth
Arlene France

Rossel Forster
Rosa Parks
Borgess Meredith
Otto Preminger
Margaret Thatcher
Casey Kasem
Gordie Howe
Bill Quakenbush
Joanne Knapp-Philo
Nigel Hollah
Stephanie Ruckstuble
Mariane Benz
Jeff Borghoff
Tracy Shorthouse
Charston Heston
Hom Shrestha
David Cassody
Tomofumi Tanno
Julie Hayden
Mdm Hui-Mei Su (Amy)
Veda Meneghetti
Peter Bery
Nina Balackova
Mryna & Norman
John McenleaV
Gwendolyn de Geest
Agnes Houstav
Daniel C. Potts

PAGE
3

DEMENTIA
HEROES
2024

94

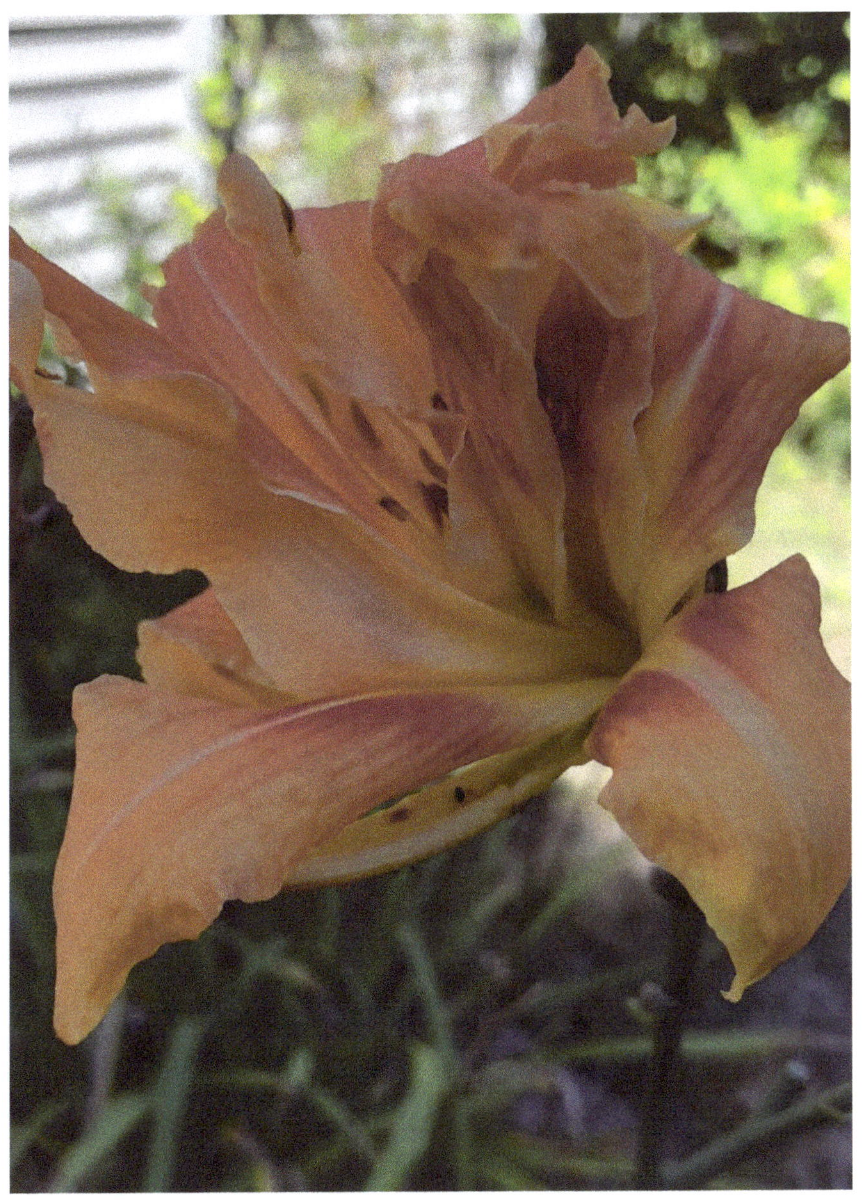